Praise for *Find*  *It*

"Andrew LeCompte shares his odyssey within ... . ugh this book, which is a compelling personal journey including more than one cult. What we can learn through his shared experiences is how vulnerable we all can be and what to watch out for when navigating through the self-help and spiritual growth universe. LeCompte knows this through first-hand and often painful lessons learned, while under the influence of modern-day gurus."

RICK ALAN ROSS
Executive Director of <u>The Cult Education Institute</u> and author of *Cults Inside Out: How People Get In and Can Get Out*

"This gripping memoir demonstrates how an intelligent man can be gradually seduced by a cult. LeCompte shows the psychological damage wrought by cultic mind control, his healing journey to recovery, and his ultimate triumph."

DR. STEVEN HASSAN
Cult Expert, author of Combatting Cult Mind Control, and Director of <u>Freedomofmind.com</u>

"This book is at once a personal journey toward love and a warning to others. Andrew's vulnerable exposé of his slow boil into a cult reveals the playbook of how coercive control masquerades as a spiritual path. A must read for anyone searching for life's answers, community, or a connection to something bigger."

SARAH EDMONDSON
Author of *Scarred: The True Story of How I Escaped NXIVM, The Cult that Bound my Life*. Whistleblower in The Critically Acclaimed HBO Series "The Vow." Co-Host with Anthony "Nippy" Ames of the Podcast "<u>Alittlbit-culty.Com</u>"

"The story is fascinating, the insights illuminating, and the writing is crisp, clear and beautiful."

KATIE BANNON
Memoirist and essayist whose work has appeared in The Washington Post, ELLE Magazine, Newsweek, Narratively, and more.

FINDING
MIRACLES
Escape from a Cult

Andrew LeCompte

Connections *Press*

Published by Connections Press, PO Box 443, Weston, MA 02493
Copyright © 2024 by Andrew LeCompte

All quotes from *A Course in Miracles* are from the *A Course in Miracles* Combined Volume Third Edition, copyright ©2007 by the Foundation for Inner Peace, 448 Ignacio Blvd., #306, Novato, CA 94949, acim.org and info@acim.org, used with permission.

Cover Photo of Andrew LeCompte by Charles Knouse
Cover Design by Adam Hay
Interior Design by Michael Vito Tosto

Library of Congress Control Number: 2023919645
ISBN: 979-8-9887483-5-9

To my son, Evan Charles LeCompte

1984-2021

Author's Note

Names and identifying characteristics of some individuals have been changed. This book represents the author's present recollections of experiences over time. Where dialogue appears, the intention was to recreate the essence of conversations rather than verbatim quotes. Others who were present might recall things differently. But this is my story.

This book is sold with the understanding that the author is not engaged in rendering medical, health, or other personal or professional services in the book. Readers should consult their own medical, health or other professional before adopting any of the suggestions in this book or drawing inferences from it.

Contents

Prologue

"No one will talk to you!"

Janet's words were still ringing in my ears as I headed straight for the men's bunk room. That was it, the final blow; I was completely shut out of the community, out of the ministry. I just needed to get my body out now. I proceeded to pull my suitcase off the high shelf of the closet, unzipped it, and began filling it with my clothes, such as they were, mostly T-shirts and a couple of pairs of blue jeans. Much less than the car full of possessions I'd had when I left New Hampshire six years ago.

Back then, I was exultant, sure that I was on the path to finding the love of God that David had promised me on the phone: Come and join our community in Utah. Find the peace of God. Sever all your special relationships, all your ties with family and friends, and come.

I had been a devoted student of *A Course in Miracles*, a spiritual text published in 1975. I had edited David's first book, *Awakening through A Course in Miracles*, and done it very well. It had become the central book of his ministry. David's having picked me for that job was proof to me that I was chosen, chosen to help David shape the words of Jesus as they came from his mouth and promulgate them to the masses in books and videos.

1

Done packing, I zipped up my suitcase and stood it by the door. I turned to look at Steven. He fleetingly caught my eye, then turned his attention to some personal items on a shelf. Sure enough, he knew I was going, yet he wouldn't even say goodbye. Just a few days earlier he had refused to give me a simple recommendation as a roommate for a place in Boston. As I stepped out of the room with my suitcase, there was Maria, one of David's Messengers. Her pretty face had not a hint of a smile this time. She looked at me with an angry glare.

"You should have told me you were leaving," she said coldly. It was like I hadn't followed orders, as I had previously been careful to do.

"You know we are moving from Utah to Mexico. You still owe us the money you said you would pay for our taxis from the airport to the Living Miracles Center in Chapala."

I pulled out my wallet and gave her the peso notes. I didn't need them anymore. I had already been coerced into giving the ministry $231,000. She didn't say, thank you. She didn't smile; she just took the money.

An Angel Walk

Formative Experiences

I could feel the heat of the fire wafting up into my face and on my bare arms and legs. At five years old I had set out to rake fall leaves to the curb and burn them as I had seen my neighbors doing. *The fire's too big!* I dropped the rake next to the burning leaves and ran up the driveway, opened the kitchen screen door, ran to the sink, and grabbed my blue plastic cup. I turned on the water and filled the cup. *Rats, this isn't much water.*

I ran back, spilling half of it, and threw the water on the fire. It made no difference. The fire was bigger and was beginning to burn the small slats of our neighbor's foot-high fence. It was out of my control. I ran back into the house, through the kitchen, and into the library where my parents were entertaining a lawyer and his wife with cocktails.

"Help! There's a fire outside" I cried.

My father rose swiftly, excused himself, and went out the kitchen door.

That evening, after the lawyer and his wife had departed, my father said, "Andrew, I have to teach you a lesson. Come with me." I followed him into the garage.

"Pull down your pants" he said, as he took a board off the pile we used for firewood.

"I was just doing what the neighbors are doing," I pleaded.

"Bend over."

I did as I was told. He held me with his left hand.

"This will teach you to never play with matches." *Whack!*

My bottom suddenly burned. *Whack!* I saw nothing but orange red.

I had the fleeting thought that, being a doctor, he knew anatomy and wouldn't hit me where it would cause long-term harm. *Whack!*

"Okay, pull your pants up."

I was crying. I pulled them up. *This isn't fair,* I thought.

As I walked back through the kitchen there was my mother, sitting at the kitchen table.

I caught her eyes and thought *Ah, she will speak up for me, console me.* But nothing. Just a sad anxious frown on her face.

I interpreted the spanking and her silence to mean not only had I done something wrong, but that I was not worthy, not worth speaking up for. My misdeed had exposed and defined who I really was. I felt a huge emptiness inside. I kept walking out of the kitchen and up to my room.

To take care of the babysitting 24/7, my parents hired a series of college girls to live in our house. They were basically uninterested in childcare, and I don't remember any of them. I was not breast fed, nor was I picked up and hugged. My mother smoked and drank alcohol, two habits she continued during her pregnancies. I later learned from my older sister that my strict Scottish grandmother had told my mother that she didn't know how to parent. My grandmother demonstrated the right thing to do when baby Tony cried by shaking him until he stopped.

The most consistent thing in my childhood, almost a sacred ritual, was cocktail hour. My parents had made a vow when they married that they would drink two dry martinis every night before dinner, The martini ritual lasted each evening from when my father got home until we could smell smoke from something burning in the kitchen. We kids could not interrupt during cocktail hour but might get an occasional cracker and cheese to mollify our hunger. I was allowed to drain the bottoms of their martini glasses and developed a taste for gin. It seemed cleaner and more refreshing than water.

There were a lot of verbal fights at our dinner table. My older brother Tony would make fun of something stupid my drunk mother said or challenge her thinking. My father would get extremely angry and come down on him with "Don't you dare talk to your mother that way!" It would escalate until Tony would jump up, run out of the room, and slam the door hard behind him. I remember thinking *Someone! Go to him! He's going to kill himself!* But I was too scared to do anything.

My brother was smarter than both of them and I could see the validity of his points but that was lost in my father's emotional violence. Pumped with three martinis and wine, my father always took my mother's side and verbally attacked my brother. I knew at some level that my father beat my brother more frequently than he beat me, but he never let me see it. He would insist that we sit and finish the meal, although I was shot through with adrenalin and had no appetite.

I also remember sitting at that table for a long time after all the others left. This was because I wasn't allowed to leave the table until I'd finished my food, which often consisted of a lump of cold spinach. My parents would watch me from the library where they were having an after-dinner brandy or whisky. When they became engrossed in conversation, I would slip it to the dog under the table.

My father had short graying hair, a sharp nose, and glasses. He usually came home late, around 7:00 pm, critical and grouchy, sometimes with blood on his shoes from doing an autopsy. He kept his tie on for dinner and every night, he had work to do. He didn't play with me unless I initiated it. Sometimes I would crawl up from behind his upholstered chair to surprise him while he was buried in his medical journals. As I peeked around the corner, he would grab me and say, "Now I got ya," and proceed to tickle me. I liked that, until he overdid it and it hurt.

One day I wrote a creative story for school about two explorers venturing into a tropical jungle to find a primitive tribe. I titled it "Me on the Menu" because the two explorers ended up being cooked in a big pot, and I thought it was great. When I showed it to my father, who scanned it quickly, he acknowledged that the title was "pretty funny," then took a pen from his shirt pocket, proceeded to mark every grammatical mistake, and handed it back to me as though that was all I had asked for. I must have been hoping for more, as my eyes welled up and I felt a sinking in my chest. I never showed him my work after that.

My mother was an attractive woman with glasses and brown hair that she usually wore in a bun. She spent a lot of time lying on her back on the couch with her arm over her face and I was constantly asking her "What can I do?" and nagging her to play with me. She rarely volunteered anything. There was no physical horsing around with her. I played a lot with toy soldiers on the floor up in the attic, setting up elaborate battle plans.

One time I was in pain in the dentist's chair and whined. My mother waited till the dentist stepped out and told me to "buck up." I had embarrassed her. She used that phrase whenever I was needy. She didn't comfort me or help me through it; she just expected me to not make noise, to not embarrass her, and to be an adult. I thought I was too soft and needed to learn to be better at hiding fear and pain. Her drinking persisted during her pregnancy, which, I believe, is why I have attention deficit disorder. I can remember the smell of alcohol on my mother's breath when she went to put me to bed.

One time I was sitting in the back seat of a cab when my father, in the passenger seat, was raging at the driver. Afterward my mother smiled and said she called him "the terrible Mister Bang" to herself. He never raged at her. My sister said that he would bottle it up and take a long walk.

I would seek out my friends, Lenny and Butch, who lived up the street to toss a football or go over to one of their houses. Butch got a BB gun, and he showed me National Rifle Association brochures for parents whose kid wanted a gun. I showed them to my parents and pressured them into getting me a BB gun. On rainy days I'd practice shooting toy rubber soldiers in the cellar. I played a lot by myself.

I couldn't stand a lot of the goody-goodies in the sixth grade. They would raise their hands and answer obvious questions, smile, and squirm happily in their seats. The teacher was really boring anyway. To break the boredom, I'd write notes and pass them to Billy. "You go bowlin' with Miss Nolan." He'd laugh, Miss Nolan would reprimand us, and make us change seats. Or I'd pull the sash on the dress of the girl sitting in front of me, then fold my hands and look like an angel. Sometimes I'd respond to the teacher's questions to get a laugh. Like: "What is the capitol of Connecticut?"

"Fartford, er ah Hartford."

I spent a lot of time in the principal's office.

At the school's recommendation, I was sent to see a child psychologist, Dr Morgan. This also was boring. I told him that I hated school and about my headaches that kept me from attending school sometimes. After I'd been to a bunch of sessions, my mother said to me: "Why, do you know what Dr Morgan asked me? He said, 'Mrs. LeCompte, do you really love your child?' And I told him, 'Of course I love my child.' You know I love you, Andrew, don't you?"

Huh? The question took me by surprise and, never having known anything different I replied, "Yes, mom, I do."

My brother, Tony, six years older than me, was infinitely cool, movie-star handsome, and a talented musician. He carpooled to Roxbury Latin School in Boston. He would come home and the first thing he would say was "Hi, where's Andy?" If I wasn't home, he'd breeze by my parents and go into the blue room to practice piano.

If I was home, he'd find me. He was the captain of his wrestling team, and he taught me to wrestle. I enjoyed wrestling him. I liked the closeness of it, the struggle, even how his body smelled. He was a middleweight but could wrestle the other team's heavyweight to a draw. One day I was really trying hard to pin him. I put all my effort and ingenuity into it, kind of folded him over, pinned his shoulders and held him down, one, two, three. I couldn't believe I won! We sat there on the rug breathing hard, and he said, "Nice job, you're really getting a lot stronger." I felt so proud of myself.

Tony also taught me to play chess. As we played, he would show me the bad moves and the good moves that could lay a trap or make a setup for checkmate. He studied the games of Kasparov and other masters in chess books. He'd say, "Don't put your knight there because, look, with these two moves I can capture your rook." We played many times and sometimes the games stretched till after dinner. Then, one evening, I beat him! Checkmate! I was in heaven.

We had a huge attic that Tony and some of his friends converted into a nightclub. He wired it himself, with a homemade dimmer switch so he could gradually lower the lights. I loved hanging out in a dark corner when there were parties. The Everly Brothers were singing "Bye Bye Love," and couples were making out on couches in a side room called the Purple Passion Pit.

Tony was good at everything. He taught me sports, like baseball and football, and even taught me to ride a motorcycle on the playground. I really loved riding on the back of his motorcycle, putting on a helmet, and strapping my arms around him as we zoomed all over different towns just for fun. He taught me how to drive a car as aggressively as the other drivers on the streets of Boston. When he was reading Gurdjieff, he talked to me about his own search for meaning. Then he went off to Harvard. My brother was a genius with an IQ approaching 160 and my father pushed him to succeed. My sister says that my father used to beat my brother a lot; I guess she could hear it. Only years later did I realize he let me beat him at wrestling and at chess to boost my ego.

I had a couple of nightmares that I still remember. In one my father was seated in his lab coat in the laboratory of the hospital where he worked. Then he turned his head in my direction and stood up with this evil grin on his face. He had just found a way to destroy the world.

In the other dream I was sitting by a campfire at night when suddenly we were under attack. An arrow came whizzing at me and my brother jumped up and caught it in his body, sacrificing himself for me.

Tony took a couple of extra years to finish his degree in math and Japanese. He came back from his adventures to visit me sporadically. One time he said he'd gotten a girl pregnant, and he asked me what to do. I was startled. I told him to talk to Dad who could arrange an abortion. He later told me that, driving back after the abortion, he and the girl heard the song "This Nearly Was Mine" on the radio and they both burst out laughing.

Another time he was returning from playing jazz trumpet and saxo-phone in New Orleans. Another time he'd been working on a shrimping boat out of San Francisco, and once he called me from Mazatlán, Mexico. After Harvard, he went to live in Japan where he learned to speak Japanese fluently. He was driven to succeed, but apparently was never satisfied. He had a restless life.

My sister Anne was four years older than me. She confirmed that my father spanked me a lot. Anne said that our last babysitter, Mary Lou, taught her how to take care of me and play with me. She told me that while Tony was gorgeous and brilliant, he was very depressed. He made a noose and hanged himself in effigy outside of Roxbury Latin School. Once he told me that when he held his girlfriend in his arms, he didn't feel love for her. This troubled me because I wanted him to find love and be happy.

I loved to get out of the house and sneak around in the woods with my bow and arrow. I was a good shot and a stealthy stalker who could nail small game, but mostly I liked just pretending I was an Indian—a scout or a sentry out to protect my tribe. I liked to soundlessly approach kids who were playing and then slip away on the sly. Even in college my roommate said he thought of me as a hunter/warrior.

One afternoon when I was in sixth grade I was walking behind the school when I saw two older kids tossing rocks and breaking the windows on one side of the school. I knew one of them was Jerry Jenkins; he was a lot older, had a perpetual sneer, greasy black hair, and a dangerous reputation. The next morning, the principal came to our classroom and asked if any of us knew anything about the breaking of the school windows. No one spoke up. He said we would not get in trouble if we told him. I raised my hand, and the principal asked me to come out into the hall. He asked, "Was it Jerry Jenkins?" and I nodded. Then I returned to my seat in the classroom as all the kids' eyes followed me.

A few days later, I was on the upper playground when suddenly I was seized from behind, held in a choking hammerlock and lifted off the ground. It was Jerry Jenkins. I pulled at his arm and kicked my legs in the air, but I couldn't get free. I couldn't breathe. I struggled; then everything went black.

Sometime later, I woke up lying on the ground with a very sore throat. I looked around and the playground was deserted. I got up unsteadily and went home. After that I never went to the upper playground again. Nor did I go up to the corner to the barber or sub shop because Jerry Jenkins hung out on that corner. I was really afraid of him, but I was ashamed and didn't tell anybody.

At the end of the sixth grade my parents gave me a choice about where I would like to go to school and they took me to visit a lot of private schools. The one I liked was the Cambridge School of Weston. It was relaxed and I liked the headmaster and the people I met. Also, Eddie, the kid next door, had been going there and he said it was great. The academic part of it was not as rigorous as Roxbury Latin and they did a lot of art and music. The kids in my neighborhood teased us that we were going to a "farm school."

So, I started carpooling to CSW. About once a week during the first year, I made the parent driving pull over so I could throw up. I don't know exactly why, probably from anxiety and secondhand cigarette smoke. The classes were small, maybe ten kids in my seventh grade, and it was generally a nice place. I was quiet and shy and a bit sad, which was fashionable among my friends there. My nickname was the "cynic." Half the kids were boarding students, largely the outplaced kids of the minor rich and famous. One of my classmates was Zanny Kaysen, who wrote *Girl Interrupted*. We kidded ourselves that McLean Mental Hospital was our graduate school.

I hung out with kids on the margin like Nes and Trevor, not the "in" kids. Nes was old enough to drive and our favorite thing was to drink and then drive into Cambridge to see if we could crash a party. One night when I was twelve, my friend Trevor slept over at my house. At my instigation we proceeded to drink hard liquor from my parents' liquor cabinet, which was in the kitchen. We mostly drank bourbon but tried just about everything else in the cabinet. Trevor wanted to smoke, and I was afraid that he'd burn the house down, so I caught the ashes in this huge metal tray. We got really drunk. The room was spinning, but I felt warm, happy and expansive.

Toward dawn, we very sincerely said goodbye to each other because we each thought we were going to die. Shortly after we lay down, he bolted for the bathroom and began retching again and again. When my parents awoke, they called his father who came and took him home. I didn't throw up and was secretly proud of my accomplishment.

I would hit the liquor cabinet every other week or so, carefully pouring the booze into a flask. One time my parents noticed that there was some bourbon missing. I told them that the next-door neighbor, Eddie, had come over and drunk it. So, my parents put a lock on the cabinet. A few nights later when they were out, I pulled the drawer at the top of the cabinet completely out and set it on a chair. Then I put my arm through where the drawer had been, reached down, and grabbed a bottle of bourbon from the top.

But again, my parents noticed that some alcohol was missing. They had marked the bottles. So, I showed them how Eddie had taken the drawer out and reached down in. I told them I'd fix it with a little carpentry. I made it so that the drawer would open but would not pull all the way out. While performing this task I took off the angle brackets underneath the countertop that attached it to the cabinet. Then all I had to do was clear the top of the cabinet, lift it off, open the drawer halfway and grab a bottle.

I was still concerned that my parents might notice the booze was disappearing, however. So, I went down into the cellar where they stored the wine and booze and took a new fifth of bourbon out of a half-empty box, took it up to my room, and hid it behind some paneling in the back of my closet. If they ever noticed anything missing after that, they never said. Years later, I found my old flask and half a bottle of vodka behind the closet paneling.

I think I drank to fill a hole in my heart. I missed love from my parents that I didn't know I was supposed to have. As a result, I felt unworthy before them and unworthy in general. My self-esteem was low. When the alcohol flowed into my brain, I felt empowered, clever, happy and ready to dance.

My last summer in high school one of our female teachers took four girls and two boys on a trip to Salamanca in Spain. The teacher would go off with the girls every day leaving me and Albert, who spoke some Spanish, to our own adventures.

We decided to go horseback riding. On the edge of town, we found Francisco Prado's horseback riding and bullfighting school. Albert and I made it known that we wanted two horses to ride out in the countryside. As we were talking about this, Francisco himself came up and said something to us about *Americanos*. Albert translated: "Because we're Americans and new to his country, he'll let us fight a bull for free."

What? I shook my head and pretended to hold reins and bounce up and down. Francisco said something else. Albert translated: "The bull's not full grown and its horns are blunted." Pause. Then Francisco said something with the word "*cobarde*," and his assistant gave a sneering laugh. I didn't need Albert to tell me that *cobarde* meant coward. *What would my brother do? He'd go for it.* "Okay," I said, "I'll fight your bull."

Soon I was standing alone in the sun, holding a red cape. There was some action at the front of the ring. Two men were standing up on either side of a solid wooden gate with long sharp poles. They proceeded to jab the poles downward, making them tremble. There was some loud bellowing from behind the gate. My knees began to shake uncontrollably. I shouted, "Don't do that!" in English, but they kept jabbing until there was a thudding noise as the big wooden door banged against its supports.

Then the gate flew open, and the angry bull charged right at the red cape I was waving at my side. The bull went right through the cape and on past me. Then he wheeled, and charged back, again going through the cape. But the next time, when he turned, he paused and looked at me. He had fought before. He charged straight at me. I took off running as fast as I could go but the bull hit me from behind and knocked me sprawling. The bull was on me with his horns and hooves. I made a desperate lurch and got behind a barrier. Was I ever glad for that barrier! I was covered in dust and bull snot, yet I felt triumphant. My only injury was a sore foot, as I had been wearing sandals.

When I got out of high school in 1966, I wanted to go to sea partly because loved Jack London's and Herman Melville's books. I signed up to join the Merchant Marine as an able-bodied seaman. The only trouble was I couldn't get on a ship. I hung out in the Boston halls of the Seafarer's International Union. No boats. So I hitchhiked out to River Rouge, next to Detroit on the Great Lakes, looking for an iron ore boat, but nothing. One afternoon I was sitting in a bar frequented by the sailors, trying to look tough when a guy said to me, "I bet you're from a western suburb of Boston." He could tell from my accent.

"See that guy pacing the floor? I'd stay away from him." The guy was wearing a sweatshirt with the sleeves torn off, his tattooed arms bulging, and he was talking loudly to himself.

"My advice to you is get back to your room before it gets dark, lock the door, and stay there."

Lying on my cot I decided that my seafaring days were over and that I would go to the University of Wisconsin in Madison, where I'd been accepted. It had a good reputation, plenty of choice of subjects and the drinking age was eighteen for beer.

My freshman year at UW I was shy and lonely. I remember waking up late one morning naked on my bed in my dorm room clutching a hubcap. I had no recollection of where my suit was, and I had a crashing headache.

Sophomore year I pledged Theta Chi fraternity and was no longer lonely. There was a lot of foolishness and a lot of drinking. My roommate, Winston, and I began having parties in our room every night for anyone who wanted to come. He had this huge cache of liquor from a chemistry department party. The chem students had all brought bottles of liquor to the party, maybe they'd had a taste, and left the nearly full bottles. Winston carried three cases up the stairs to our room. What a goldmine!

The University of Wisconsin in Madison was an excellent institution. It had a fair number of radical, left-wing faculty members, such as the anti-war political activist Harvey Goldberg, professor of history. I loved their anti-establishment lectures and how they practically applied their ideas to our society, of which I was highly critical.

In October 1967, I was on my way to French class when I heard a large group of students chanting, "One, two, three, four, we don't want your fucking war." As I was a member of the Committee to End the War in Vietnam, I knew these students were protesting Dow Chemical, maker of napalm, interviewing on campus. I joined them. Police in riot gear formed lines with shields that the students broke through. Then there was tear gas and cops beating students with clubs. Eventually, the police cleared the area. Many of the students had to go to the hospital. I was shaken and angry and went to the student union to hear our leaders speak about the war and the political situation.

In a lot of ways, I had no respect for the American "establishment." I studied how our capitalist system did anything for profit; that ours was an imperialist country where those in power lied to the nation and brought us blindly into foreign wars against innocent people. It was as if the country was run by cold-hearted, mean men like my father. I hated our culture and liked to think of myself as more European than American.

Then one morning at 6:00 a.m. I heard the phone ringing in the upstairs hallway. I felt a sudden dread, nausea in my stomach.

"Andy, it's for you." No one ever called me on the telephone, especially early in the morning.

My breathing became constricted.

On the line my father told me my brother had committed suicide in Hawaii. He had run a hose from the exhaust pipe into the car. The car was still running when the police found him.

I sat on the fraying carpet after the call. I'd vaguely been expecting it, knowing how tormented he'd been. Nonetheless, now that it was here, my mind was careening around. Now that I'd lost my idol, what was my so-much-lesser life about? Not much. I really loved him and was always hoping to be with him on a cool adventure. Well, that wasn't going to happen.

My parents and sister came to a hotel in Madison a block from the frat house. They talked about Tony and how he and I had had the closest relationship in the family, but in general, talking with them was not a healing experience. None of us could talk about our emotions. No one cried. I think they all felt uncomfortable and a little guilty about Tony. They were fright-ened by his intellect and his intensity. They couldn't accept him. They couldn't love him.

That night, I shared a room with my father. Thinking about how much I loved my brother and how much he loved me, I began to cry in my bed. My father called out thinly in the darkness, "Andy, are you okay?"

"Yes," I replied and stopped crying.

After my brother's death I went into a stupor of alcohol and depression. If suicide was his choice, and he was a talented genius, suicide was the best I could look forward to. Life sucked. I was in existential despair. I read existential works by Jean-Paul Sartre and Albert Camus. The United States was fighting an insane war. I read about it. I read *The Wretched of the Earth* by Marxist psychiatrist Frantz Fanon and learned about the economic and psychological ravages of French colonialism. I empathized with the colonized and had nothing to look forward to.

2.

Rebirth

In the summer of 1968, I hitchhiked around Europe, and crossed from Spain to Tangier, Morocco on the ferry. My intention was to crawl off and die in a cave somewhere in Morocco or Algeria. I thought this would be a romantic and gallant way to go that would make my brother smile. I rode the Marrakesh Express train from Casablanca to Marrakesh, high as a kite on some really excellent hashish I'd picked up in Tangier.

The next day at noon, no one was stirring in the usually bustling medina or main square of Marrakesh. I remembered, with a wry smile, that only mad dogs and Englishmen would be out under the hot midday sun. The scent of exotic spices floated into my nostrils. Then I heard some light laughter floating from the far side of the square. I headed toward it through the shimmering heat and was delighted to find a young American couple in an animated exchange with a Moroccan. Both sides were making valiant attempts at communicating, repeating phrases, and using hand gestures. But each attempt was followed by open-handed shrugs and good-natured laughter.

The Adlers, I learned, were on a break from the Peace Corps in Guinea, and just wanted to enjoy Morocco. The Moroccan, Joe, was an electrician on vacation who wanted to show them the sights. I saw their good intentions and their frustration. Joe spoke Arabic, Berber, and French, but no English. They spoke only English. Ah ha! I spoke French and English. I seized my moment and began interpreting between them. Suddenly I was the catalyst, the one who could translate (and make jokes on either side). They welcomed me heartily. The four of us decided to join up and travel together, which we did for ten blissful days.

We had fantastic meals seasoned with cumin, a spice I'd never tasted before. We heard musicians playing the twangy, three-stringed "sinter," high-pitched warbly singers and colorful exotic dancers, male and female. We had fresh-squeezed orange juice and pastry every morning for breakfast. We rented bicycles and toured gardens, museums, and old French Foreign Legion fortresses. Joe got us great discounts on thick, colorful Moroccan rugs.

My black mood on life gradually shifted from wanting to crawl off and die to discovering that I could be happy, funny, and really appreciated. I was the life of the party. In a short time, I came to love the Adlers and to be loved by them. I would have loved having them as family.

Debra Adler was brunette, very attractive, and wore rather short dresses, I thought, for being in the Middle East. But she was obviously a tourist with a husband, John, who looked and dressed a little like Harrison Ford in *Raiders of the Lost Ark*. Some evenings John would retire to the hotel early, as he had periodic fevers from something he'd picked up in Guinea. We had an understanding that I would be her protector when he was not around.

Debra and I especially hit it off on those evenings. One night, as the city cooled and quieted, we went through winding streets to dinner at a small restaurant where we heard traditional soft *maw-wal* vocal music floating out the open door. The lighting was subdued, and each table was lit by a candle. The host, assuming we were a married couple, seated us in a cushioned nook with a canopy over it. After we had eaten, Debra took a poem out of her purse. She held it near the candlelight and read it to me. It was a beautiful poem by Pablo Neruda with vivid, sensual language. Then she turned to me, the candlelight reflecting in her eyes, and said, "Andy, John neglects the back of my neck."

I hesitated. I so wanted to accept the implied invitation to kiss her neck. She uncrossed her legs and leaned a little toward me. Yet I didn't want to violate an unspoken agreement of fair dealing I had with John, who was admittedly a great guy. "You should tell him," I replied.

The day I was to fly to Algeria approached. I had a ticket, but I didn't really want to go. The Algerians had recently driven out the French colonists in the late fifties and early sixties, and the country was still unstable. I had made the flight reservation back when I was in my bleak frame of mind. I had wanted to introduce something exotic into my dismal life. Maybe I had bitten off more than I could chew. The Adlers were headed off in another direction. So, the next day I went to Casablanca to await my plane. Joe had given all of us the name of a bartender in Casablanca as a possible, but unlikely, way to meet up sometime in the future.

In Casablanca I found the bartender in a not-so-great bar (not Rick's *Café Americain* by a long shot) and told him where I was staying. Then I went back to my room and lay down on the bed, entertaining thoughts of dying in Algeria. Shortly after the war, a white person with the name Le-Compte might well get tossed into prison. What a crazy idea.

The room smelled of insecticide. I lay there rigid, pondering my fate. Suddenly I caught the distant sound of laughter, then a voice calling my name. Sure enough, it was the Adlers! I felt saved! It was so glorious to hear them and be with them again. They had had a change of plans. I ditched my plans for Algeria. This meeting with the Adlers felt lifesaving to me. I, who had arrived on the brink of self-destruction, with abysmally low self-esteem, was in their eyes a delightful companion, both highly entertaining and trustworthy. This was my first miraculous experience.

I decided my life was definitely worth living. These great people really liked and appreciated me. In a sense, that was my coming-of-age story. Rather than suicide, I would emulate my brother's earlier life, be a good student, search for and find a more loving and satis-fying way to live together with people.

The Adlers and I stayed in close touch. Later, when their son was born, they asked me to be his godfather, which I happily accepted. I loved babysitting for him. As he matured, in keeping with my god-father role, I got him some of my favorite books, such as *Siddhartha* by Herman Hesse and *Autobiography of a Yogi* by Paramahansa Yogananda. My interest in spirituality had started with discussions I had with my brother about life. He had been searching for love and truth beyond everyday existence. I felt the quest was mine to further and hopefully complete.

Even more than being my loving brother, Tony had been my guiding mentor. I saw him suffer as he sought to find meaning for his life in the emotional desert of my family. And he shared his thoughts with me. He was concerned for me. The trouble was that I was six years younger. That was a lot. He would tell me about his existential studies and experiences, but I could grasp only the general drift. He told me about his psychedelic experiences with mushrooms and other drugs, but his final message to me was emphatic: drugs had brought him more misery than benefit. So, I never tried anything stronger than hashish.

It was my Moroccan experience that led me to study about the French colonization in North Africa and the messianic rebellions against the French. Lacking the military power of France, masses of Berbers and Arabs gravitated to *mahdis,* charismatic spiritual leaders who promised them a golden age and that the French bullets would turn to water as they fired them; unfortunately for them, that did not prove to be the case.

Jump to the summer of 1974. I was reading about the Mamluk Turks in Widener Library at Harvard in preparation for my oral exams in history at UCLA. One evening I met Martha at a contra dance at the Cambridge YWCA. She was quite short, with slightly frizzy brown-and-gold hair pulled back in a braid. She was light on her feet, bobbed slightly to the music and, when swinging, looked her partner right in the eyes. She was a great dancer and knew everyone in the local folk music and dancing scenes.

Martha introduced me to Transcendental Meditation at the Meditation Center on Garden Street. Transcendental Meditation is a form of silent mantra meditation developed by Maharishi Mahesh Yogi. The TM technique involves the use of an internally voiced sound called mantra and is practiced for fifteen to twenty minutes twice per day.

After my initiation, I experienced a mental calmness that allowed me to view my life from a broader perspective. Meditation offered me a mental healing, slowing me down, letting me realize there was peace and content-ment in this very moment, in spite of what was whirling around in the world outside. I didn't realize until decades later that it was a cult

I appreciated the fellowships I had been getting at UCLA. But I realized I had no intrinsic interest in studying for my doctorate in Middle Eastern history. I had been reading to prepare for my exams and couldn't have been more bored. Grad school had been useful to keep me out of the war in Vietnam. That threat was now passed. So, I quit graduate studies, drove back to LA, got my belongings, and drove back again to Massachusetts.

I became a waiter at Ferdinand's Restaurant in Harvard Square, and it was fun. It seemed as if even the lowliest busboy had a master's degree. In my twice-daily Transcendental Meditation practice, I would find a place where I could sit quietly and undisturbed. I typically chose a straight-backed chair so I could keep my back straight and notice if my head started to fall forward in sleep. I would close my eyes and become aware of my breathing. After a minute or so I would begin silently repeating my mantra, a two-syllable Sanskrit phrase which had been given to me for its vibrational quality. I would repeat the mantra gently for twenty minutes. That was it.

Sometimes during meditation, I would transcend the present moment completely, leaving my mind and its constant internal dialogue behind. These were moments of total peace. Then I would come back to the awareness of the room where I was and that I was thinking again. I could remember nothing except I knew I hadn't been thinking and that it was a wonderfully nurturing experience. The positive experience with meditation predisposed me to look favorably on spirituality as a solution to life's difficulties.

In my new mindset, I became a highly competent waiter. If a large drunken party suddenly descended on the restaurant, it was given to me, because I could remember all their orders and keep my cool if they started to get rowdy. If they insulted me, I could stay steady, see the bigger picture and laughingly cajole them into better behavior.

One of the other waiters did some teaching at a private school. Remembering how bored I had been in school, I felt I could bring some fresh air to teaching. I wanted to be a different kind of teacher, one who was alert and alive, who really engaged students in interesting topics. The path that was open to me was substitute teaching in Cambridge and I signed up. My results were mixed. When the students were interested in learning and I had a good lesson plan, it was highly enjoyable. I also brought some of my own amusing activities to divert them when needed.

There was a marked difference, however, in the quality of the schools. One morning I was called to a school in Central Square. The building was old and fairly run down. I reported to the principal, who looked at me a little doubtfully as he told me "You'll be taking Mr. Fitzgerald's classroom." A teacher led me to the classroom, saying "They're a feisty bunch," and shut the door behind me as the bell rang.

Most of the students were running around poking each other and laughing. There was a tall kid holding a wallet up high with one hand and a smaller kid jumping for it and whining. I loudly said,

"Okay, please take your seats." Only a few of them paid attention and did so. There was a clutch of kids in the corner, whom I approached. As I got up to them, they backed up a little, casting sidelong glances at each other. Then, fast as a gunslinger, one kid hit another in the face, dropped his hands and put on a face of innocence. Right in front of me! The kid who was hit put his hands over his face to hide that he was crying.

"Hey," I said, "hitting is not acceptable. We're going to see the principal." To my surprise the hitter came along easily enough. In his office, the principal seemed to doubt or minimize what I was saying. The hitter, whose name was Johnny, was relaxed with a blank face. The principal said to me, "Johnny's mother has spoken to me and to members of the School Committee saying that teachers were singling out Johnny for punishment." "Johnny, if I send you back to the classroom, will you promise to behave for the substitute teacher the rest of the day?"

Johnny gave a soft "Yes, sir" and that was it. I took him back and, after much shouting, got the students to sit down. I began reading aloud an adventure story I'd brought with me about some kids their age and gradually things settled down.

I was pleased to discover I had a knack for teaching. but I wanted to teach students who wanted to learn. And I wanted to teach in an environment conducive to learning and personal development rather than to keeping order.

3

Growth Through Adventure

Still a meditator, I took a job as a teacher at Saint Anne's School for girls in Arlington Heights, Massachusetts. There I taught "at risk" girls English, French, history, and special odyssey programs which included a field trip to Washington, DC. Many of the girls had been referred by the courts for drug use and petty criminal offences. They were at risk of running away, doing drugs, or stealing. The Episcopal nuns who ran the school were quite progressive about education and ran a lovingly tight ship. Classes were small. Nonetheless the girls were a tough bunch of inner-city kids, not interested in abstract academics. I felt compassion for them and wanted to get through to them.

To my surprise and delight, the school had just finished building a high ropes course for experiential learning. It included such challenges for students as climbing a rope ladder to a small platform high in the treetops and then tightrope walking along a cable to a second tree while holding on to a higher cable for balance. All the while the student was in a harness connected to a safety belay rope such that, if they fell off the cable, they would be caught by their belayer and slowly lowered to the ground.

I enjoyed teaching outdoor adventure education to this group of students. The girls were much more responsive outside than they were in the classroom. Many of them became enthusiastic about taking risks and exerting themselves way beyond what they would normally have expected of themselves. I enjoyed seeing them grow in self-esteem as they overcame their fear of heights and learned to trust each other and the person who had them on belay. They encouraged each other to go for it and offered each other reassurance, becoming a mutual support group. This amazed and pleased me.

One day I was positioned aloft in the trees. I had just clipped in the last girl and sent her down the zip line when the lunch bell rang. I decided to ride the zip line down myself. I reached up and clipped my harness to the cable. Then I reached for the handles and started down, picking up speed rapidly.

Crunch! I came to a dead stop on the wire. I was left swinging forward and back in the air. The wheel above me that rode on the cable had ground to a halt. Gradually my swinging stopped, and I was able to take in my situation. The wheel mechanism had broken, and the wheel would not turn. The harness around my waist was attached to the cable so that if I got tired holding on and let go, it would catch me. But the trouble with hanging by your waist is that, after a while, you can no longer breathe.

The girls and my co-teacher looked up at me in horror, mouths open. I had to get down! No room for a firetruck back here. *Oh shit.* Didn't want to look as panicked as I was. Then I got an idea. I raised my legs and pulled myself up with my arms. Then I whipped my legs downward while at the same time snapping my arms forward. The stuck wheel jumped down an inch on the cable. Hallelujah! I continued the same maneuver what seemed like a hundred times until they could reach me from a stepladder. I was exhausted and my heart was beating wildly. But, so as not to frighten the girls, I calmly walked into the lunchroom, sat down, and stared at my plate of food until the next bell rang.

I had some things in common with these girls. I had grown up feeling unloved and with low self-esteem. I was also a little smaller, weaker, and less confident than my peers. That changed markedly after I went to a loving summer camp in Maine. The staff there seemed to have been selected for their ability to care about and inspire young people. There, over three summers, I learned to swim, run, and canoe with the best of them.

I remember, Ray, the counselor in charge of the waterfront on the lake challenging me to race a female counselor to see if I could break the camp's eight-lap freestyle record. *Yes, I can do this.* We both dived in when he blew the whistle. In the first three laps, under the water, I could see the female counselor falling behind. Then I focused on maintaining a fast rhythm. I was going like hell, watching my left arm descend into the green water trailing bubbles and pulling, then looking up under the other armpit as my face broke the sunny surface and I sucked in a breath. I was exultant. I ended up clobbering the speed record and enjoyed being the best in camp, with my name painted on the swim-record board.

I also really loved the three-day canoe trips and sleeping overnight in the woods. Several times paddling in the stern I had to power and steer the canoe into a hard headwind whipping up whitecaps, while a less powerful person in the bow did their best to keep up. I liked carrying the heavy wooden Old Town canoes on my shoulder as we portaged between lakes. I got stronger and I was developing a taste for adventure.

Remembering how great my bullfighting and camping experiences had been, and now, seeing how much the outdoor adventure program was benefitting the girls at St. Anne's, I began searching for an Outward Bound program in which I could really prove myself. I was delighted to find an outdoor adventure program designed for teachers of students with special needs. Oscar Jennings, the program leader, was quoted in the flyer saying it would be physically demanding, so I spent the summer running and swimming to get in shape.

I met up with the group and Oscar led us through some get-to-know-you exercises. Oscar was tall, tan, muscular and wore a ponytail. The group then started out on a three-week trek across the High Peaks of the Adirondacks: rock climbing, mountaineering, marathon running and whitewater canoeing. The Adirondack Park, a "forever wild" state park in northern New York State has an area of 6.1 million square miles, making it bigger than Yellowstone, Yosemite, Glacier, Grand Canyon and Great Smokies national parks combined.

We began on the east side of the Adirondack Park in Keene Valley, which boasts some truly impressive sheer rock faces. The leaders set up a belay from the top of one of them. I looked to be one of the fittest of our group and was selected to be the first to scale the rock face. I felt honored. I went up carefully, one handhold and one foothold at a time, until I got halfway up and couldn't see any more handholds or footholds within reach. There was a distantly possible foothold up off on my right side, which I might have been able to reach with a big kick. But the extension was so far that it would pull my left foot off, and if I didn't land solidly with my right foot, I would be left dangling in the middle.

Some of those below chanted "Go for it!" and others cried out "Yeah!"

Easy for them to say. I was scared. I went for it.

I kicked my right foot out and up as high as I could—but didn't make the foothold. I was left hanging on the rock face by my fingertips. After about fifteen excruciating seconds, during which I was terrified I was going to die, my fingertips peeled off the rock and I fell, calling out "Falling!" as I went. I was afraid I'd crash on the bottom of the cliff, but to my surprise I was caught on the belay rope, swung there from my harness, and then was slowly let down. *Thank God!* I sat out of sight behind some big boulders as my madly pumping heart and hard breathing slowed down. I thought to myself, *Nobody's going to make it.*

But after a while a voice called out, "Suzie made it!" I could hardly believe it, although Suzie was in good physical shape. Next, they called out "Babette made it!" This I couldn't even imagine because Babette was not in good physical condition. I walked back to the group and learned that the women were taking a different route up the rock face. Nonetheless, it was a lesson in humility for me.

Oscar then told us that we were going to take a two-day hike along a mountain ridge. He used the words "shakedown" and "winnowing" as he described it. We put on our packs and Oscar set a quick pace during the ascent, requiring us to take rest stops to catch our breath. Then we followed a narrow trail along the ridgeline that had steep drops on alternate sides.

One of the women fell forward on her face and froze. Afraid to move, thinking if she rolled her pack off the wrong way, she'd fall off the cliff to her death, she began to scream, "Help me I went to her, put my hand on her shoulder, assured her she was safe, and she was able to sit up. The next day we were all a little wobbly. Another woman, who was in poor shape, sprained her ankle. As we climbed down off the ridge, Oscar and his co-leader helped the two who were having difficulty. These two were unable to continue and were driven to a hospital. I must say the idea of relaxing in a clean hospital bed had its appeal.

Our next adventure was to take a special three-day expedition, without our leaders, through a trackless wilderness called the McIntyre Range. Seven of us started out early in the morning during a thunderstorm. We fought our way uphill through densely packed spruce trees, the lower branches of which were dead, with sharp, interlaced points, so the lead person had to break them off to make it passable for the others. The branches still managed to shred our sleeping rolls, a fair amount of our clothing, and scratch our heads, arms, and legs. If the dismal climb was not taxing enough, we were inundated with swarms of mosquitoes, constantly buzzing and feeding on us.

As the hours went by, people began to lose it. Pam fell into a concealed hole up to her hip and burst into tears. I helped her up and comforted her. In another hour it appeared we were completely lost, and spirits sank. Dan, our biggest and strongest, began screaming obscenities and throwing big branches into the woods.

A thought came to me, and I found a tall white pine. "Hey, Dan," I called out. "I have an idea how to get out of here. Give me ten fingers."

With his boost I climbed the tree so I could locate the peaks of the range and took some bearings with my compass. Then on the map I set a direction that would get us to the gap between the peaks. Just before it got pitch dark, we got through the narrow pass and managed to set up our two little tents on a small patch of level ground on the other side.

In the evening I unrolled my sleeping bag and crawled in, completely wiped out. But then I heard laughter coming from the other tent. I couldn't believe it. I went over and stuck my head in the tent flap. There was Annie laying out some dirty wet socks and talking with the others.

"How come you're feeling so good?" I asked.

"I knew you'd pull us through," she replied.

Wow, really? Me? I'm glad you did.

The next day one of the women was completely exhausted; she could barely walk. We couldn't leave her there, so I took her pack and strapped it on top of my own. We started down and, halfway through the morning, found a trail. Yay! But the stress was wearing on us, and we had a long way down. Frank lost it. He began screaming, "I'm hungry" and ran ahead down the mountain until he came to a little stream with a pool. He pulled off his pack and began to eat energy bars.

I came down and joined him by a pool. I was tired and dying of thirst. I bent down to drink out of the pool, forgetting I was still carrying the packs. The weight of the packs was about 120 pounds, and they pushed my head and shoulders under the water and embedded my face in the bottom. There I was, stuck, with my head underwater and unable to push myself up.

Oh shit, I can't breathe, I thought. *Wouldn't it be funny for the others to come down and find me drowned in a pool of water?* I wasn't at all afraid, just amused by the situation. I knew I was still the master of the situation.

I kicked my legs to the right and was able to roll over onto some rocks, slip out of the packs, and get up. Eventually we did make it down and found the program leaders. When we told them how strenuous our ordeal had been, the assistant leader subtly turned to Oscar and, raising his eyebrows in surprise, made a soft whistle.

Every morning we'd get up at dawn and "run and dip." This meant we would run until we found a pond or stream, take off our clothes, or not, and jump in the water. One day we ran up and down five-thousand-foot Mount Algonquin. Another day we ran a marathon through the woods. I twisted my ankle and had to limp back while I was attacked by clouds of loudly buzzing, viciously biting deer flies. In the experience, I hated it, but was later pleased with how I was becoming tougher.

Next, we did three-day fasting solos in the woods. Oscar described it as purifying and like going on a vision quest as was done in some American Indian tribes. I picked a remote wilderness spot beside a small stream. For three days and nights I stayed in that spot, watching the stream flow by. I got to know all the currents and eddies, the places where the water bubbled below a rock. And I had plenty of time to think about the adventures of the past few days, about girls, like Suzie, about my life in general, all of which was pretty good. I heard, then noticed a chickadee on the lower branches of a balsam tree. Some dark clouds came over and there was light rain for a while. I was amazed at how my mood darkened with the weather. After a while it brightened up and so did I.

After about six hours I got hungry, but after two more hours the sensation of hunger went away. Then hunger would come by in waves, gradually getting further apart. I began to feel weak and dizzy, but then that too passed. I got into my sleeping bag when it got dark and listened to the stream and rustling of some small animals as I drifted off to sleep.

On the second day my hunger had passed, and I was left just feeling lighter. I went to sleep that night and suddenly I was wrestling a bear with long teeth and claws. A voice called to the bear in Spanish, and it immediately stopped fighting. The bear sauntered off. I woke up, realized it was a dream and saw that I had rolled my sleeping bag a couple feet and was up against a bush. I wondered if the dream had meaning. I had spent a summer in Spain, but this semi-hallucinogenic episode mostly reminded me of Carlos Castaneda's book *Don Juan: A Yaqui Way of Knowledge*. I thought of it as possibly foreshadowing experiences to come.

By the third day I was feeling really good, enormously grateful for my life and all the people in it, very happy to be alive. I have since learned that fasting can induce a euphoric state called ketosis. When I joined the others we introduced food to our systems slowly, some yogurt and fruit. It was so delicious! This was an experience of sustained peace that I could either be still with or move around and hug people. I realized that in a short time I had come to trust and appreciate these people. I decided I was going to seek out euphoric spiritual experiences like this in the future.

That blissful feeling persisted as we embarked on the final leg of our journey across the Adirondacks to its western edge. We paddled across Tupper Lake in canoes, then descended the Racquet River, shooting the rapids as we went. I had become quite skilled handling a paddle during summer camp, so this part of the trip held no feeling of fear for me. I just felt exuberant. The river and all its variety of rushing, crashing currents was beautiful. As luck would have it, we ended up at Jamestown Falls, not far from my parents' Adirondack cabin, but I chose not to break up the spell of my trip by visiting them.

At the end we processed our experience and gave each other feedback. Suzie, by far the most attractive girl on the trip, with short brown hair, a wholesome face and shorts, talked about how happy she was with her rock-climbing and canoeing accomplishments. Then Oscar, the charismatic leader, insinuated that he had slept with Suzie during her solo. Suzie glared at him, her face turning red, and she hissed, "Damn it, you promised." Oscar gave a little laugh and asked the next person about their trip.

When my turn came, to my surprise each member of the group pointed out something that I had done to help them or the group. Annie said she could relax knowing I was there. Frank said, "I've never followed anybody in my life, but I would follow Andy anywhere." I was genuinely surprised by all the praise! I felt happy, content and seasoned, like I could go anywhere and do anything I wanted to.

This was the peak experience of my life to date. As I grew and developed, I found I loved helping people grow and develop their skills and confidence. These were the sort of thing that a loving, attentive father would do for his child. I also liked living communally

with this group of people, sharing the daily tasks of cooking and eating, and the more spiritual/loving connection that developed between us.

That fall I took a job teaching geography in a public junior high
school in Reading, Massachusetts. The overall experience of the
school turned out to be about controlling the kids, with little room
left over for fostering student curiosity. Between classes, teachers
were required to stand at attention outside their classrooms and en-
force the no-talking and no-running rules. Inside the classroom students weren't supposed to sit at one another's desks.

I had fun taking the kids outside to practice orienteering with
map and compass. I set up an obstacle field and had the kids follow
the orienteering directions to traverse it. I told them that, if they
went off course, they'd hit a mine field. They paid close attention and
were making it through the course surprisingly well. Kenny, a bit
overweight and crew cut, was one of the last to go through. Suddenly
he realized he was off course, shouted "Blam!" threw his arms up,
jumped and fell as if he'd just been blown up by a landmine. He did
being blown up so well, we howled with laughter.

I also had the students learn to make maps. For this I had them
work in groups of three. As they collaborated, they worked out some
disagreements about the scale of miles and what should go where on
the map. At one point the vice principal stuck his head in the room
and the students fell silent. "Let's keep it down in here," he said and
closed the door.

For my infractions, I was called into the principal's office. The
principal was a former marine who had been brought into this junior
high school to restore control. His office was spartan—just a desk,

bare except for the school calendar and him sitting behind it, his bald head reflecting in the fluorescent lights. He informed me that there were to be no more small groups, each student must be at his own desk, and that candy wrappers had been found on the floor of my classroom.

"See that this doesn't happen again, Mr. LeCompte," he said menacingly.

"Yes, sir."

Over the following months he managed to squeeze much of the joy out of teaching. To make matters worse I had moved to Reading so I wouldn't have to fight traffic every morning. I became really bored in that apartment, finding amusement chasing cockroaches with a blowtorch, amazed how it could burn off their legs in one pass as they tried to run away.

I left that school after one year and took a job as a development associate with a small nonprofit economic development company in East Cambridge. The interesting part of that was learning to be a grant writer, and to my amazement, see money come in to start development projects.

4.

Searching for Community

I wanted to move from my lonely Reading outpost into Cambridge. Reflecting on how much I had enjoyed growing tight with the Specially Bound group, I decided to look for a way to live a communal lifestyle in Cambridge. I yearned for a sense of community and connection.

I searched for the right mix of people through a co-op housing network. At one of the network's meetings, I met a group of four people who were laughing and obviously really liked each other. They liked me too, and I soon moved into Porterhaus, off Porter Square. As a communal household, the five of us rotated who did the shopping, the cooking, the dishes, and the cleaning.

My new friend Peter Slowkowski was an excellent cook. Sometimes he would cook *galumpkis*, which are Polish cabbage rolls stuffed with ground beef, tomatoes, red wine, olive oil and spices. They were delicious.

Peter was an amazing guy. For example, when the dishwasher broke. Peter took it apart, spreading the parts out all over the kitchen floor. Then he reassembled it and it worked perfectly. This was all the more remarkable because Peter was blind. He also used to beat me playing chess. It was a warm, loving household full of interesting conversations and fun games. We attended parties at other houses as a group and would pick up the pace of the dancing. And the parties that we threw at Porterhaus were notorious for being terrific fun.

Sometimes Peter and I would head over to the liquor store to pick up a bottle of Eclipse Barbados rum. We did quirky things together, like attend the annual Kielbasa Festival in Chicopee wearing the festival red T-shirts. I found that I was happier living in Porterhaus than I had ever been.

Then Peter took advantage of a special computer training program for people with visual impairment. It was in Connecticut, and he was gone for many months. I think either I resented his going or thought somehow that our losing communication was a sign he didn't really like me. It was a self-fulfilling prophecy. I didn't call him during that time and some alienation and resentment built up. Our friendship was never the same. I still regret it.

Meanwhile, the development associate job dried up and I became a real estate broker in Cambridge. It was fun learning how to do it, but I found that a sales job just wasn't my thing.

Buoyed with the warmth of Porterhaus, I decided it was time to look within and choose an occupation that really spoke to my heart. I wanted direction and encouragement in my life. After much searching, I finally found the ideal program, a customizable master's degree program in humanistic psychology and organization development at Associates for Human Resources (AHR) in Concord, Massachusetts. Organization Development practitioners help organizations go through positive change, including everything from strategic planning down to effective management and supervision.

My study program included applying the principles of the Gestalt Psychotherapy of Fritz Pearls and the client-centered therapy of Carl Rogers to people in group situations, principally their workplaces. The faculty was composed of gestalt psychotherapists, various body/mind therapists, and some well-known organizational consultants. I made the most of it, fully developing my research projects and participating energetically in all different kinds of therapy.

In his book, *On Becoming a Person*, Carl Rogers describes the healing power of unconditional positive regard. He validated something most of us know from personal experience, that it feels incredibly good to be listened to and understood by someone who sees only the good in us. His ideas resonated deeply with me. I wanted personal confirmation that I was a good person, and I wanted to experience this in my relationships with others.

I experimented with various forms of bodywork, such as Rolfing. Rolfing is a powerful physical therapy experience that physically reorganizes the connective tissues, called fascia, that permeate the body. When we're stressed our muscles tense, and if they stay that way over time, the fascia attaches, and we remain more or less locked in that position. My Rolfer was Jeff Johnson, and he had an unerring eye when it came to sizing up my body. I went through ten sessions, during which Jeff's strong hands tore away the adhered fascia on my muscles and bones. This was acutely painful. At the time Jeff's practice was at the end of a dead-end street. I'm convinced that was to minimize the number of people who would hear his patients' screams. But the pain stopped instantly, and I was left with a straighter spine, a delightful freedom of movement in my limbs, and even a wider cranium.

As part of my degree program, I did a one-year internship at

Digital Equipment Corporation, where I learned to use the Myers-Briggs Type Indicator. This psychological tool helped people identify the strengths and weaknesses of their personality and gain insight into how they tended to behave as team players. Of sixteen possible personality types, my type was ENFP, which stands for extroverted, intuitive, feeling, and perceiving. This type is spontaneous, creative, enthusiastic, caring, and people-pleasing. I went on to use the Myers Briggs Type Indicator in corporations to facilitate team building and with individuals to help them find the career field and position in which they would flourish.

In my AHR program I met a woman from Iowa, Emily, my student adviser actually. She had straight, long blond hair, a rather narrow head, and full lips. After a few weeks I began to be interested in her. She really took the alternative healing methods we were studying to heart and rejected the traditional medical model espoused by my father. We broke the ice one evening drinking beer at a tavern in Concord with some fellow students and had our first kiss the next day walking around Walden Pond.

Where I was extroverted, Emily was introverted. When there was an important decision, she took her cues from inside her mind rather than from others, and when she made up her mind she dug in her heels. She was extremely spiritual in her own esoteric way. I heard her remark to some friends, "I just don't belong on this planet." I noticed it but I let that little flag go right on by me.

We moved into an apartment together, the downstairs of a semi-rural house, but our relationship was not going well. Emily and I didn't communicate well with each other, which is ironic in that we were both in a human development program. We often saw situations differently. We tended to swallow our upsets and annoyances with each other and let them smolder. I experienced Emily as strong-minded and fierce in defending her point of view when she cared about an outcome, which wasn't pleasant when we were at odds over something. The relationship was so uncomfortable that I was seriously thinking of ending it.

At this time, I took "est" (Erhard Seminars Training), a confrontational and demanding program that challenged participants to critically examine themselves and go beyond their normal limits. The est leader essentially convinced me that *I* was responsible for everything that happened in my social world, primarily the dysfunction in my relationship with Emily. I became convinced that I personally could change myself so dramatically as to make our relationship work. So, rather than split up, I decided to marry her. Oops. Bad idea. Probably sensing my mistake, I got really drunk at our wedding. We went on a honeymoon in Greece and, under the influence of ouzo, conceived on the last day. This was 1983 and I was thirty-five.

Evan's birth was truly a miracle to me. I felt awe and wonder holding this tiny but complete human life in my hands. He was a unique person, with eyes that saw me, and a voice to express his feelings. I marveled at his tiny, perfect features, his breathing and was intoxicated by his new-baby smell.

Emily, however, suffered a major case of postpartum depression. She was brooding. Even though Evan was colicky and crying incessantly, she wouldn't allow anyone to come into the house to help. She turned away friends and babysitters. This created a major problem for me. I would come home from my organizational development job, find them both crying, and have to take the screaming child from her while she went to sleep. I took him on long walks in the neighborhood, often singing softly to him, until he would finally quiet down and fall asleep.

One night she got up when Evan started crying. I thought she would take care of him and went back to sleep, only to be awakened by her ear-splitting shriek. I thought, in terror, she had swung him against the radiator and dashed out his brains. But when I came into the baby's room, he was okay, just sliding off her lap. I picked him up and comforted him. Emily was looking off and didn't appear to be fully alert. Our situation was becoming untenable, and I was worried.

I was busy at work creating a day-long management skills training program for hospital department heads. The program was very well received, and I taught it in hospitals around the country. But driving to work in the morning on only three hours of sleep, I would imagine pulling into a motel off the highway, calling in sick to work, and sleeping all day. It was an extremely demanding situation, and I couldn't handle it by myself. I was at my limit. I longed for the communal support I had had at Porterhaus, but we had sold the house.

A friend told me about a spiritual community of about forty people, the Emissaries of Divine Light in Exeter, New Hampshire. He gave me one of their brochures that read: "Since 1932, Emissaries of Divine Light have been helping people worldwide deepen their attunement with the universal wisdom and love within them. We aspire to bring humanity together to create a spiritual regeneration of the Earth."

I lit up when I read that. I wanted to attune to the universal wisdom and love within me, and this community just might provide the "village" needed to raise my child and provide support for my beleaguered wife. Also, I thought that this might be just the type of spiritual group that would appeal to Emily. So, I called and made an appointment to visit.

As I drove into the property, I saw the ice had not yet gone out on a small pond. A young woman in dirty jeans met me and pointed out the two large farmhouses, additional newer buildings, and a large barn, that served to stable the two big draft horses still used to plow their large organic farm. She told me about half the people worked on the property and half worked in various places nearby.

Then I was introduced to the leader of the community, a mild-mannered man in his sixties, with short gray hair and a clean-shaven sharp chin. Seated in front of a cheery fire in the fireplace, he explained that the "attunement" referred to in the brochure involved having a man skilled in this procedure stand behind you while you were seated and cup his hands on each side of your head. Then he would silently attune your inner vibratory field with the universal love vibration. I had more than a little skepticism but knew it would appeal to Emily.

This sounded like just what I was looking for. I explained my situation and how Emily and I could use support and then said, "I'd like to bring my family to live here."

"Wow, that's wonderful," he said, "but we don't allow people to move in right off the bat. We like to get to know each other over a period of time first. You could, however, move nearby and come over every day for meals and activities if you like."

As I drove home, I was a little disappointed about not being able to move right in, but I also saw a bright side. I had just gotten a well-paying organization and management development job at Signal Capital Company in Hampton, New Hampshire. If I bought a house in Exeter, my commute to work would be short. From our AHR experience I knew Emily believed in body work and the power of healing energy to be transferred from one person to another through the hands.

When I got home, I said to Emily, "Sit down. I have something to tell you."

She sat down hesitantly with her mouth slightly open. Later she told me she thought I was going to say I wanted to divorce her. I told her we were going to move to New Hampshire to join a spiritual community, a place that shared spiritual values like hers. She was greatly relieved. We talked about it, and she came onboard. It sounded to her like just what she needed.

We attended the Sunday services and liked them. Soon we bought a brand-new house not far from the community. It was a colonial-style house with clapboards and shutters. I made a sandbox for Evan and planted a few hemlock trees. We moved in and I hoped life would be better joining the community and living in the new house. We went over there frequently for communal meals and attunements. We both participated enthusiastically. They had a men's weekend, and I told an African coming-of-age story about a young man who defeats a tiger to the encircled men in front of a blazing fire by the pond.

But Emily and I still didn't know how to communicate with each other. Perhaps she was still suffering from postpartum depression.

Where I felt it most acutely was around our parenting of little Evan. When he was old enough to walk around, she began telling him what not to do. She would get angry with him and once complained that he had no remorse for doing things wrong and that he would end up a criminal. Developmentally, her expectation was way beyond what was possible for a child at this age.

Late one afternoon I was coming upstairs from the garage in my three-piece suit after my workday at a finance company in Hampton. Emily opened the door at the head of the stairs and swept a big load of kitchen dust and debris onto me. No explanation. I thought *This is it!* Emily had made some positive connections in the community, and this provided the backup plan I needed. She told me she didn't want Evan coming to sleep in our bed anymore and I thought, *No it will be you who's not sleeping in my bed.* Soon after I told her that I wanted a divorce. She was not opposed.

As we approached divorce, Emily moved into the Divine Light community itself while I stayed in the house. She latched on to one of the leading men there, George. We passed Evan back and forth and when he was two, had him attend a Montessori school. I enjoyed playing with him on the living room rug. He would get a running start and jump on me; we would roll around laughing.

Apart from playing with Evan, however, I was sad and miserable. I felt like the hollow shell of a man. It annoyed me that she seemed to look down on me from her position on George's arm. I decided, largely for Evan's benefit, that I had to pull myself together. I had been taking care of my psychological needs by drinking bourbon and attending psychotherapy. My therapist recommended that I join CODA (Codependents Anonymous) and Al-Anon. Codependents Anonymous because it was clear I needed help in choosing female partners. Al-Anon because it was clear that my parents were alcoholics. I went because I was down and desperate.

In a group setting, I was always attracted to the most dysfunctional girl in the room. One girl I found especially attractive had long golden-brown hair, dressed very well, yet had a sullen expression on her handsome face. When she told her story, I was amazed to hear that her brother, as a way to get back at their parents for all kinds of reasons, took a rifle and, from a distance, shot the big gas tank on the side of the house. The explosion obliterated the entire house, which fortunately was empty at the time. This sort of dysfunction in a woman's life attracted me more than repelled me. I could understand her inner pain; I thought I could help. There was a vulnerability that also drew me. Maybe this extended from my desire to save my older brother and being too young to do anything for him.

When Emily's and my house was sold, I also moved into the community. It was awkward to be living in the same community with my estranged wife. There were other kids and farm animals for Evan to play with. Most of the single men lived in a bunch of small rooms in the basement of one large house. I didn't spend a whole lot of time there as I commuted to my job in Hampton every day. It was nice to come back to the community, change out of a suit into jeans and a sweatshirt. Sometimes I would go out dancing, either contra dancing in a nearby town or rock-and-roll dancing in Portsmouth. There were opportunities for me to have sexual relationships but I'm rather conservative in that area and technically I was still married.

Like some other intentional communities, Emissaries of Divine Light had its good points, such as communal meals, and its less obvious not-so-good points: is seemed to me that certain male leaders had their way with the women. On several occasions I remember looking up out of the basement window and seeing one of the leaders walking toward the upstairs door, followed by the rhythmic pounding of the bed in the room of one of the younger women. Her husband had moved out of the community six months prior. The senior men, it seems, serviced the resident women according to a code I never stayed long enough to learn. I wasn't comfortable seeing Emily every day with George. I felt lonely but being in a community with a lot of nice people and eating common meals helped. That was until I found out one of the women we used as a babysitter for Evan was spanking him. Not okay with me. Evan and I moved into an apartment in Exeter with a young couple and their kids. Evan attended the first grade in Exeter, an excellent school, and I shared custody with Emily.

5

Alcoholics Anonymous Leads to
A Course in Miracles

Still trying to feel better after the split-up with Emily, and thinking my alcoholic parents were to blame for my core unhappiness, I attended an Adult Children of Alcoholics program at the Caron residential treatment center in Pennsylvania. I participated for the first two days, telling my group and the counselors how my parents abused alcohol. I mentioned that I, on the other hand, didn't misuse alcohol. I told them more about my skillful and measured use of alcohol. I was a little proud of it.

On the third day, however, a counselor held up a bottle and addressed me and alcohol as if we were two people. She said to me that alcohol was my best friend, the one who was always there for me, the one who never let me down. No matter how bad I felt, she always eased my pain. I was effectively married to alcohol.

I reflected. Yes, I had always managed to fortify myself with a few stiff drinks before social occasions. It certainly helped me to kick off the dancing. If there wasn't booze at the party, I always had my flask. I had done a zillion stupid things when I was drunk and was lucky not to have killed myself or others. I'd had some of the world's biggest hangovers. The counselor interrupted my reflections: "Admit it. You're an alcoholic"

She had me. I was an alcoholic. I'd come to Al-Anon because of my parents' drinking. But the program had shown me that *I* was an alcoholic. I was angry, angry at my parents for practically raising me on booze, angry that I was stuck in an addicted self, and angry at the staff for nailing me. The counselors and other participants seemed used to upset reactions and smiled calmly at me. Back in my room that night I opened the window and stuck my head out. I began screaming at the top of my lungs. I'm not sure what I shouted, but it wasn't pretty. After several minutes, I paused and looked at the walkways below, lit by small lampposts. There were men in tuxedos and women in long dresses and glittering jewelry all headed to the building across the quad. I had chosen the evening of their big fund-raiser for my outburst, but they all were taking it in stride.

My roommate, whom I knew was an experienced alcoholic, came in with a couple books. He talked to me for a while in a friendly, supportive way. He was a comforting presence. He gave me a small black book of daily prayers called *Twenty-Four Hours a Day,* and he told me about how the AA program worked and how it had saved his life. Then he showed me his copy of "The Big Book" of Alcoholics Anonymous. Over the next several days, the counselors and participants at the Caron Foundation took good care of me and launched me as a member of AA.

Back home in Exeter, New Hampshire, in September 1990, I went to my first AA meeting, and I was really nervous. There is a stigma to being an alcoholic. Everybody knows that alcoholics are dirty bums, living on park benches, drinking booze out of brown pa-per bags. But a guy came up to me, welcomed me, and brought me over to the coffee machine and some doughnuts. I took some and sat down in the back.

A woman started telling her story. She was well dressed, the wife of a minister, and she spoke openly of how her alcoholism had been ruining her life. She described in some detail how, a few years ago, with her "fortified" coffee, she had managed to pass out during coffee hour at church, and worse episodes. Now she expressed sincere gratitude for the AA program that kept her sober. Alcohol hadn't ruined my life—yet, but I could identify with her. I went to more meetings. These people welcomed me and understood me at a deep level; they too had felt the compulsive need to drink, to shift their inner reality to one that was less painful. I felt like I was home. After a while I told my story and was warmly received. I accepted that I was a binge alcoholic. I used alcohol to free up my dancing and to alter my mood. I remembered that one time when I was feeling very much alone in Reading with no one to call on a Saturday night, I killed a fifth of Jim Beam. The hangover all the next day almost killed me. I should say that I was an alcoholic now in recovery. I never took another drink after my first meeting. I was more aware of my general feeling of unworthiness in social situations. But I went to ninety AA meetings in ninety days and worked AA's twelve steps.

One day, I went to an AA meeting in Portsmouth, New Hampshire with a different agenda. I had something that I hadn't admitted to anyone—that I had had suicidal thoughts. I was still feeling empty after divorcing Emily even though I still saw her every week to pass Evan back and forth. She seemed to be content in her new relationship. Me, nothing. I didn't have a suicide plan, but life sucked. I would wonder if maybe I should follow my brother's example.

It was a fairly large meeting, about thirty people. I was sure that when I mentioned suicide everyone would back up against the walls in shock and horror. In this regard I knew my condition was much more serious than any of theirs. So, I got up there, anxiously, and, as part of my story, I said I had had suicidal thoughts, then took my seat. The meeting ended, and I was afraid to look around. I stood up to go but two men came up to me, both smiling. They said they had had suicidal thoughts also, that it was part of our alcoholic "stinking thinking" and not unusual. They seemed to like me more for having confessed this dreadful thing. Suddenly, it didn't seem so overwhelming, and I felt connected. They were my kind of people.

Phil, whom I met in A.A. meetings in Portsmouth, was a wonderful, loving man. He cried when he told his story about how his alcoholic father had died on the kitchen floor in front of him and his mother. He had hugged his mother and said, as a boy of six, that now he would take care of her. I wanted to have his big heart and his vulnerability. When I asked him to be my sponsor, he said, "I'd be honored to be your sponsor." He was a great sponsor. I participated in tons of AA meetings and study groups. Alcohol no longer tempted me. I've been sober since September 7, 1990. However, I've seen many who tried to become sober and did not make it, which is a very sad thing.

An estimated one in eight deaths among adults is attributable to excessive alcohol use. The program laid out in the Alcoholics Anonymous Big Book has about a 50 percent success rate, and another 25 remain sober after some relapses. I believe that AA is so successful in combating this addiction because it is a loving, spiritual program that offers connection to a supportive community. This was the beginning of me living a spiritual life including prayer on a daily basis. Step three says we "Made a decision to turn our will and our lives over to the care of God as we understood Him." I confessed to my sponsor that I didn't really like God, was a bit afraid he'd judge me and condemn me.

Phil said, "He's not like that."

"How do you know?"

"Well, Andy, try this: imagine it was your job to design God. What would he be like?"

"Well for starters he wouldn't be judgmental. He would be loving and supportive no matter what I did." That's really the main thing for me.

Phil said, "Guess what. That's him!

"But what about the wrathful God in the Bible who fries whole tribes?"

We're not talking about the Bible at all. We're talking about the God of your understanding. You just told me you understand God to be loving and supportive. You've got it!

I had to let that sink in. Then I sat back and smiled.

AA's steps four and five asked me to make a searching fearless moral inventory of myself and share the exact nature of my wrongs with God and another human being.

I told Phil things I was embarrassed about, like masturbating outside a girls' dorm after a date.

He'd smile and ask a few questions such as "Did anyone see you?" No, "Was anyone harmed?" No.

He'd shake his head and say, "Andy, that's really nothing."

"Once when I was ten, I pushed a girl down in the snow and she hit her head on a rock. Her father was so angry he wanted to fight me."

"Was everything okay the next day?"

"Yeah."

"Did she suffer any serious harm?"

"A bump on the head."

"Is that all?"

"Yeah"

He looked me right in the eye. "Andy, you're forgiven."

And I felt forgiven. I crossed it off my list of transgressions, many of which I'd done while I was drunk. I think I made an amend or two when it seemed appropriate, and then my list was done. I felt happy, much lighter, I gave and received a hug from Phil.

He had internalized love's essence: a deep, kindly acceptance of other people and himself.

Phil and the AA program brought me through all twelve steps. They are all great. The last two steps say: "Sought through prayer and meditation to improve our conscious contact with God as we understood Him, praying only for knowledge of His will for us and the power to carry that out." Now I could genuinely pray to God and not feel like a hypocrite. The twelfth step is "Having had a spiritual awakening as the result of these steps, we tried to carry this message to alcoholics, and to practice these principles in all our affairs." Wow, a spiritual awakening! That must refer to how I was becoming more confident and content. I was genuinely helpful to new guys who came into the program. One of them asked me to be his sponsor and I accepted. I was a good sponsor; helping people grow and become happier was my thing.

Prior to AA I felt I was different from other people, and I was. I was spiritually vacant and behaviorally erratic. I covered it up pretty well, but after practicing the twelve steps and being in the brother/sisterhood of the AA program for a few years I became more emotionally stable. Phil was the first man with whom I could be completely honest, and he became a good friend. I also had a benevolent God of my understanding, whom I trusted. And I was glad to be able to help other alcoholics gain and keep their sobriety. It's hard to overestimate the power of Alcoholics Anonymous.

Phil was also a student of *A Course in Miracles,* a spiritual self-study program designed to awaken people to the truth of our oneness with God and love, and I began attending Course meeting with him in addition to the twelve-step meetings. I went with him because I wanted what he had, a happy acceptance of life. I wanted his warm self-confidence in telling the story of his own mistakes in life, as a completely loving and accepting parent would. And he extended that love to me. It initially seemed very dense, academic, and convoluted, but I hung in there, attended ACIM discussion groups, and read the entire twelve hundred pages several times over the next few years. Eventually, I found that it had a consistent, authoritative voice. And it fascinated me.

Phil's AA sponsor, Cecil, a gentle, very handsome man of Finnish descent, attended these meetings with us. Although there is no one to make such a designation, to my mind Cecil was a Master of *A Course in Miracles.* He had read the entire Course a dozen times and marked his current copy up with pens and colored markers. This was his second copy. Every morning when he woke up Cecil would do one of the Course Lessons, which were approximately a page a day. Then he would read a section in the Course Text, which was sometimes quite extensive, and meditate on it. In fact, that was basically all he did all day, follow the Course.

Cecil didn't work and was separated from his wife. Although they got along well, she sued him for child support; still, he wouldn't get a job. He was doing what he believed the Holy Spirit of the Course was telling him to do. Finally, since he didn't have any assets, the judge had him do a few days in jail, but Cecil was unfazed by it. He would go to meetings with Phil, Beth and me and then we would all go and have Chinese food at a restaurant on the coast and discuss the ideas presented in the Course. Beth was another student of the Course who was also motivated by the camaraderie and the learning. I used to love those long afternoon meetings: the cozy seating, the great food, a view of the ocean, relaxed discussion, and the waiter bringing us pot after pot of hot tea.

After I completed my master's degree from AHR, I obtained various management and organizational-development positions, first in a national health service company and then in a national financial services company. I really enjoyed designing programs and interventions that would help employees in the company work more happily and efficiently. I continually strove to help them learn to communicate more humanely with each other. I taught managers and executives to motivate with enthusiasm and kindness rather than threats. I taught employees how to resolve conflicts and productively confront their bosses.

I made some nice connection too. Once, when I was giving a second seminar to hospital department heads in Minnesota, a supervisor said she had put the key points of my first seminar up inside her locker and read them every morning for inspiration. A national association in Florida asked me to put on a stress management program for them two years in a row. The second year, to my surprise, one of the managers from my previous program came again. He said the program was so good the first time he wanted to do it again.

When the finance company I was working for was taken over by a huge bank, I left the corporate world and became a life coach, helping people to obtain their personal and professional goals. My clients found me to be good at motivating them to succeed. This was ironic because my own life was still in tatters from my divorce. I had to stop crying and wash my face before they arrived.

6

Compassionate Communication

One thing I did for my personal self-care was learn to play the alto recorder and in the summer of 1994, my music teacher gave me a video of Marshall Rosenberg demonstrating Non-Violent Communication. Craggy old Marshall was playing the part of the dying father of a cute young woman wearing a denim jacket and jeans. Father and daughter had never spoken of the sexual abuse that he had perpetrated on her when she was much younger. When she confronted him about it in this simulation, he said, "I was alone and weak during that year. Fired from my job. Your mother was away in Venezuela."

"But how could you do that to me?"

"I'm so sorry I hurt you. I guess it was a way for me to feel close to you."

"But it was a betrayal! You really wounded me!"

"Are you angry because you need to know that I really love you? I do now and I did then."

She paused, then said "Yeah" more softly and wiped her eyes.

Watching, I was mad at the father, and amazed that Marshall could empathically get into the father's place and speak the words the father hadn't been able to.

I wanted to learn Marshall's communication skills. In particular, I wanted to learn how to listen empathically to another person in the deep way he could. It felt like the missing puzzle piece in my family, a social scientific way to connect at a feeling and heart level, even, or especially when there was profound disagreement. So, I called Marshall and arranged to attend his first international teacher training in Switzerland.

I loved every minute of the program. Marshall taught people to own their feelings and needs in conflict situations, without blaming the other person. When I got home, I began using Non-Violent Communication in my training and consulting work. I realized, however, that Marshall's mode of communication made the speaker sound needy. I could see how to make some dramatic improvements in the program. What exactly was it important for me to teach? An important personal value began to crystalize for me—to love, to be loved, and help other people learn how to love each other.

I practiced this heartfelt communication with Evan, and it flowed easily. I moved around a fair amount in New Hampshire and across the river in Maine, but I always made sure he had his own comfortable room. One of his teachers gave me a piece he had written about me. In it, he talked about the activities we did together and how he enjoyed being in his room and hearing me in the kitchen cooking up one of his favorite foods. He closed with, "I have a great dad."

One crisp fall evening in 1998 I was looking to get out and have some fun, so, I went to a traditional New England contradance in a grange hall in Eliot, Maine. The caller had a loud, warm voice, and the band was made up of a fiddle, guitar, flute, and other assorted instruments. It was a high-energy dance, and the place was humming. I noticed a very attractive woman with long blonde hair who appeared to be a very smooth dancer and had a friendly smile. I asked her for the next dance, and we hit it off, maintaining a lot of eye contact. I enjoyed holding her fit body as we swung to the music.

When the band played a waltz, we had the opportunity to talk into each other's ears as we slowly circled the room. Her name was Melissa, and I was eager to get to know her better.

In my organizational development work, I frequently used the Myers-Briggs Type Indicator and wanted to know Melissa's type. Not to put her on the spot, I volunteered, "I don't know if you're familiar with it, but I'm an ENFP on the Myers-Briggs Type Indicator." She started to laugh and replied, "I'm an INFP. I'm a clinical psychologist and I use the Myers-Briggs Type Indicator all the time in my work."

Our personalities had three factors in common, the N, F, and P, which stand for intuitive, feeling and perceiving. This generally makes for a relatively easy couple relationship. But we differed on the E for extroversion and the I for introversion. Introverts enjoy their private time and are more likely to keep their thoughts to themselves, unless asked. At the end of the dance, we exchanged more information and I found out that she lived and worked in Dover, New Hampshire.

One winter night we went out to eat at an Indian restaurant in Portsmouth. She had a fairly long ride back to Dover and she hadn't yet come to my place. After dinner we began to make out in the entryway to the Indian restaurant. We stayed there an inordinate amount of time kissing and hugging. The waiters flipped the lights on and off a few times as it got later, and they wanted to close.

Finally, we got the message and as we left for the night, I saw the waiters smiling and laughing.

On Valentine's Day I took her out to dinner in Dover. Afterward, we went back to her place and made out on the bed. It was sensational! We went to more dances together and fell in love.

Each of us had had a bad prior marriage. My marriage to Emily had been over for about ten years and Melissa's had been over for a similar amount of time. I wanted to get married and here was a lovely person with whom I could enjoy intimate, empathic communication. I skipped over the fact that she was an introvert and proposed to her. She said yes. Melissa, Evan, and I moved into a spacious apartment on Miller Avenue in Portsmouth.

Professionally, I devoted several years to refining my empathic communication techniques and integrating them into my consulting practice with couples and groups. Then I pulled it all together to write a book. I would jump out of bed every morning, go straight to my computer and start typing. I was onto a breakthrough. The book was published in 2000, entitled *Creating Harmonious Relationships, A Practical Guide to the Power of True Empathy*. Here is a brief example of how it works.

A nursing director named Sylvia came to see me. She looked haggard; there were dark circles under her eyes. She told me they'd had a big fight during a staff meeting that really upset her.

"I'm afraid I did the wrong thing; I feel terrible about it. If only Tom wasn't such a jerk."

I asked her to tell me what happened.

"Well, we had a code blue, a cardiac emergency, which happens, but we didn't get the defibrillator working as soon as we should have.

I had a staff meeting right afterwards. Tom got in my face, all oppositional. I told him off. He really aggravates me sometimes, and I don't know what to do with him."

I told Sylvia she could learn a better way to handle challenging situations like that, and she agreed to work with me on her communication skills.

She called me a couple of weeks later and said she just had another staff meeting and she'd handled Tom better. "We had a code blue and almost lost a patient. Tom accused me of not doing my job. He was practically shouting," she said.

"What did you say? Run the conversation by me."

Sylvia smiled and said, "I told Tom, 'It sounds like you're really *angry* about what happened.'

"'You bet I am!' he said.

"I guessed, 'Is it clear who's supposed to do what at shift change?'

"'Yeah, but we're understaffed and asked to do the impossible.'

"'Would you like more help at shift change?'

"'I sure would.'

"I want you to have the support you need, let's talk about it.'

"OK, let's.

"And we talked for probably half an hour. We each agreed to some changes."

"You did a good job guessing at his positive hope for support," I said.

"Yeah, I guess I did. The change in him was amazing. He went from being angry to cooperative," she said with a smile.

This was my reward: to help people be able to resolve conflicts and communicate in a more compassionate way. True empathy is connecting with another person's feelings and hopes. It was something I hadn't experienced from my parents as a child.

I had told her that the easiest way to connect with a person's feeling is to guess what emotion might be going on inside them. In Tom's case Sylvia guessed correctly that his emotion was anger. If she had been wrong, Tom would have corrected her.

Then she guessed at Tom's hopes, the positive desires motivating a person. Tom hoped to be respected (a freedom hope) and to get more support at shift change (a connection hope). Hopes can be seen as aspects of love, or as divine attributes. They are the good intentions inside all of us, and because we are all essentially the same, we all share the same hopes.

I learned that I couldn't get my hopes met at anyone else's expense. To do so would negate my hopes for connection. This is why forcing or coercing another person does not bring happiness, which is found through mutual cooperation. Given the interconnectedness of hopes, either we both get our hopes met or neither of us does. My being heard and understood means that I feel better and am more ready to listen and empathize with you.

I know this because, as I have worked with hundreds of people over many years, I have found that we are always doing our best to get our hopes met, no matter how unskillfully. Given this understanding, my guiding attitude toward other people has become, "You have a good intention and I want to find it."

My book was well received in popular and professional circles. Teachers used it to teach interpersonal communication to college students. Psychotherapists used it in their client groups. Couples used it to improve their relationships. The book sold out and was even translated into Turkish. I had discovered a more effective way to communicate in emotionally challenging circumstances. Teaching people how to use this method is close to my heart, and I refer to the whole model as compassionate communication.

The heart of it, empathic listening, has become a core value. It is about connecting with other people at a heart level. It provides a way to connect in love. I dedicated that book to my father, and I wish he had read it at the time of my birth. His motto was "Children should be seen and not heard." I believe this gaping hole in my childhood sparked my passion to learn and teach how to express love.

With this mindset, I have reflected on my childhood. My father put great pressure on Tony to perform academically. Tony searched with desperation for meaning in his life apart from achievement. I remember his interest in existentialism and his reading authors like Kierkegaard, Gurdjieff and Lady Murasaki's *The Tale of Genji*. He learned Japanese. He experimented with hallucinogenic drugs at Harvard with Richard Alpert (the future Ram Dass) and Timothy Leary. With them, I believe he learned to manufacture LSD. I know he had flashbacks from drugs which only exacerbated his depression.

A year or so ago my sister Anne told me that Tony was probably gay, but he could never tell that to our father. That seems accurate in hindsight. I feel even more compassion for Tony, who wanted my father to be proud of him, yet had to hide this central aspect of who he was, quite a predicament in a household with alcoholic parents who didn't know how to love their children. Apparently, Tony had a male lover in Japan, a very nice photographer, whom I later met in Toronto. How I wish that Tony was still alive.

7.

The Attraction of the Course

Despite marrying well, writing a book, and succeeding professionally, I still felt incomplete. I had a professional lull and had plenty of time to think. I felt a yearning for a deeper experience, for a higher knowledge about life. I wanted to become more loving and wiser.

Believing that *A Course in Miracles* must be the source of Phil's love, I tore into the book, hoping to become more like Phil. At first, in the early 1990s, I found ACIM to be difficult reading. The writing style was ponderous and complex, yet I persevered and in about eighteen months of reading and going to the meetings with Phil and Cecil, I had become an ardent student of the Course. The book itself was transcribed by Helen Schucman and William Thetford, two research psychologists at Columbia. Helen, the principal scribe, attributed the words to Jesus Christ. Since its publication in 1975, *A Course in Miracles* has sold over two million copies and been translated into twenty-seven languages.

The acim.org website says, "A Course in Miracles (ACIM) is a unique spiritual self-study program designed to awaken us to the truth of our oneness with God and Love." As I studied the Course over the next two decades, I became completely convinced that this was indeed the voice of Jesus. It lined up with "The Life and Teachings of Jesus," which is the last section of another classic spiritual text, *The Urantia Book*, first published in 1955 in Chicago.

The pages of my ACIM book became covered with underlinings, notes and highlighting on every page. Each time I went through the book I underlined or highlighted in a different color. Frequently the sentences were long, even convoluted, but they were completely coherent, and the Course didn't contradict itself. The writing is not linear. It has been described both negatively, as inaccessible to the majority of people, and positively, as poetic and symphonic, with themes weaving in and out. Much of it is written in a Shakespearean, iambic pentameter rhythm.

The metaphysics of the Course are more Buddhist than Christian. Our origination is described like this: All was one in eternity, all was Love, but the Son of God fell asleep and dreamed he had separated from God. This dream was so terrifying that the Son made the physical world as a place to hide and fragmented himself into all the people in it. The way back to Love is through forgiveness, to let go of false judgments of others and rediscover our essential oneness. Through forgiveness the thinking of the world is reversed. Forgetting all our misperceptions, and with nothing from the past to hold us back, we awake and can remember God, When we are ready, God himself will take the final step in our return to him.

I accepted this as the truth.

I wanted to return to the love of God. I wanted to be filled with a bright, euphoric love. *Return to Love* is the title of Marianne Williamson's highly popular book. She is a well-known charismatic leader in spiritual and religiously progressive circles. Reading her book and listening to her talks on audio cassette made me even more certain in my quest to learn the Course. It also appealed to the rebel part of me that wanted to do something that was counter to the prevailing culture.

Actually, the prevailing culture in my house growing up was my father's militant atheism. Whenever God, Jesus or the Bible came up my father would ridicule it. He was a heartless man. At a deep subliminal level, I craved love, and if, indeed, a loving God existed, I wanted to do whatever it took to find him.

I recited Course lessons such as these:

"God is but Love, and therefore so am I." *Wow, I am love. I so want to experience that.*

"God, being Love, is also happiness." *Yes, I dearly want to be genuinely, completely happy.* "There is no love but God's." *I have tried loving girlfriends and wives, and they weren't it, that kind of love doesn't last*

"I feel the Love of God within me now." And I began to imagine the feel of the love of God within me. I soaked it up. I could begin to sense it. At last, I had found the love that would grow inside me, extend through me and radiate out from me!

And the path to realizing this love was quite attainable. I need merely commit myself to the acceptance of God's plan for me and the Holy Spirit would do the rest. When I balked at the amount of difficult reading the Course required, Phil pointed out this paragraph:

Once you accept His plan as the one function that you would fulfill, there will be nothing else the Holy Spirit will not arrange for you without your effort. He will go before you making straight your path and leaving in your way no stones to trip on, and no obstacles to bar your way. Nothing you need will be denied you. Not one seeming difficulty but will melt away before you reach it. You need take thought for nothing, careless of everything except the only purpose that you would fulfill. ACIM, T-20.IV

So, it would become effortless. I wanted the Holy Spirit to help me find the love of God. With total devotion to Him it seemed quite doable, and I began to develop a new spiritual identity.

The Course answers the question "What am I?" in this way:

I am God's Son, complete and healed and whole, shining in the reflection of His Love. In me is His creation sanctified and guaranteed eternal life. In me is love perfected, fear impossible, and joy established without opposite. I am the holy home of God Himself. I am the Heaven where His Love resides. I am His holy Sinlessness Itself, for in my purity abides His Own. ACIM, W-pII.14.1:1-6

I memorized this and said it to myself over and over again, often on long walks in the woods. I began to think of myself as the Son of God, awakening to his true self. This spiritual path was becoming extremely attractive.

During my early years with the Course, the 1990s, I was a pastoral associate and board member at South Church, Unitarian Universalist in Portsmouth, where the minister taught me how to pray with someone. Prior to studying A Course in Miracles, hospitals and death had frightened me. A Course in Miracles, on the other hand, says flat out "there is no death," and through my deep study of the Course, I had come to believe it.

One of my duties as a pastoral associate was to visit with people in the hospital. I visited with Ed in a Boston hospital. He was slowly dying of AIDS. I was feeling very confident as I entered his room, and I asked the two guests who were with him to please leave while Ed and I prayed. Then I talked with Ed for a while and got a feeling for what his spiritual beliefs were. He was really tired of being sick for so long with no positive outcome on the horizon. So, I took his hand and talked to him in prayer about his having lived a good life, about his love for his family and friends, his wish to be at peace, and that his spirit would not die. Then I asked for a period of silence.

After a few minutes I gave his hand a squeeze and Ed slowly looked up at me. Then he said, "You know, Andy, that is the first time I have felt really peaceful since I first got sick." He was very grateful, and I knew he meant it. Then I went out and invited his friends back in.

Three weeks later I was called to Ed's bedside again. This time he was in intensive care. He had chosen to undergo chemotherapy for kidney cancer. I knew right off that, in his weakened condition from AIDS, curing the kidney cancer was not the reason why he had chosen to have this chemotherapy. He wanted something that would bring a quick end to his suffering. He was belted to the bed with restraints on his arms and legs and a clear mask over his face that was spattered with blood he had coughed up. His eyes were closed. Periodically his body was wracked with a spasm, his back would arch up and he let out a sharp groan. His family members were standing around the room with their backs to the walls in fear. I walked right up to Ed and put my hand on his bare forearm and started talking to him. He calmed only slightly. I told them that he could hear and that he loved them and would like them to talk to him.

I said to his family members, "Ed loves you and he can hear you. Step forward, put your hand on him and speak to him." Several of them tentatively did so and then the rest moved closer, speaking endearments and touching him or the bed.

I began to sing Amazing Grace and the family members joined in, each to his ability. Then I switched to loudly humming the tune and they hummed along. Each of them shared their love and hopes with Ed, some just in whispers. I remained in the room until all of the family members had a hand on Ed and his spasms lessened. I felt great, as if Jesus or the Holy Spirit was indeed right there with me extending peace and love to all present. I thought to myself, *Wow, I just performed a miracle.* Then I had to leave for another appointment. But I went feeling happy and surprisingly powerful.

Not long after that, I learned that Ed found his eternal peace. I later learned that the way I had transformed that fearful situation into loving connection had deeply affected the family and they were very grateful. So was my minister.

I also discovered the Course-related Attitudinal Healing work of Dr. Jerry Jampolsky. Attitudinal Healing is a way of healing that helps remove self-imposed blocks such as blame, shame and self-condemnation that stand in the way of experiencing peace, love, and happiness. It is based on the belief that it is not people or experiences outside of ourselves that cause us to be upset. Rather, it is our thoughts, attitudes, and judgments about them that cause us distress. Health is defined as inner peace and healing as the letting go of fear. I was welcomed at several Attitudinal Healing conventions as a presenter and my workshop sessions received great reviews. Jerry was kind enough to endorse my book before it came out in 2000.

My main focus at the time was on my program of compassionate communication, using my own book. I was very successful right from the beginning thanks to my state-of-the art web site which was built by my son. I taught conflict resolution to many local groups and interpersonal communication in local colleges. I then trained a small group of trainers from the University of Maine to co-facilitate my new program, which I trademarked as "Let's Talk." We presented programs to corporate executives and managers all over the country. This consulting practice was quite lucrative, and I grew a nest egg that I put into investments. But in 2008 as a result of economic depression, my training and consulting work dried up.

During this time, without other practical application, my enthusiasm for *A Course in Miracles* began to wane. I hadn't experienced any more miracle-like experiences. Phil had moved to another state, and I wasn't going to as many meetings.

In 2006, however, my attention and enthusiasm were rekindled when I read the book *The Disappearance of the Universe* by Gary Renard. Although it uses the literary device of Gary's conversations with visiting ascended masters, the book recasts the teachings of the Course in simple language. For example, "There really isn't anyone else out there. There is only one ego appearing as many."

Gary was selling his book at an ACIM conference in Massachusetts. I was also there with a dozen copies of my book, *Creating Harmonious Relationships*, which I wanted well-known students of the

Course to read. I chose to give them away, so cost would not be an obstacle. Several of them subsequently wrote favorable reviews of my book. Over the next few months, I also got to know him and his exciting book.

I flew to Costa Rica and spent a week with Gary Renard studying his book, *Disappearance of the Universe*. I knew his book so well I remembered lines from it that even Gary had forgotten. One time when we were walking to lunch, I said something about spirit, and, in an unguarded moment, he said, "Yeah, I could use that." *Hold it,* I thought. *If he could use something I suggested, then the source of his material was not purely the ascended masters as he claimed in his book.* This cast some doubt for me upon the authenticity of his writings.

During a break, we went to the biggest, highest zip line I had ever seen stretching from one mountain across a wide valley to another mountain. I could hardly believe it. I was scared, but I noticed that Gary didn't appear to be. I thought if he can do it, then the Holy Spirit will save me too. So, I got into a harness, took a leap of faith, and had the ride of my life. It was like being a hawk gliding over this valley with a tiny river rushing way below. When we both were on solid ground again Gary and I had a big hug. After the program Gary said I knew his book so well I could have taught it myself.

After my book was completed, I had two nagging thoughts. One was that I couldn't live up to this high standard for empathic communication that I had set. I noticed that I rarely guessed at another person's feelings and hopes or used other parts of the communication model I had proposed. The other was that I had written a description to demonstrate my negative judgment, taking my friend

Phil from AA as an example. When the book was in print, I read this part over with all my off-the-cuff negative judgments about Phil and saw that I had gone too far. I had implied he was ugly, a poor dresser and not very bright. Unfortunately, a negative judgment doesn't just disappear. I wanted to take it back, but the books were already being sent out to reviewers. I felt massively guilty about it. I even rolled on the floor whining about it.

Melissa was coaching me and said all the right things, but I was still full of guilt. It became clear to Melissa that I was depressed. This felt right to me; depression ran in my family, at least as far back as my grandfather, who was hospitalized for it. My brother had been depressed before he committed suicide.

So, I started going to regular psychotherapy sessions and taking the prescribed antidepressants, which brought me to a subdued normal. My book was published, but I didn't want to market it. This was part of my fear that other people wouldn't like me. I also had an aversion to selling myself. The one exception was going to a book signing at Barnes and Noble in San Francisco. That was a lot of fun. I also had fun using the book in the various workshops and seminars that I taught in corporations and to community groups.

Melissa and I were married in 1999 and we bought a house in the woods outside Dover, New Hampshire. We hired a contractor to open up the interior plan of the house and put in a gas fireplace. He only completed three-quarters of the work, so I finished it myself. I remember feeling good standing on a ladder attaching new clapboards around the chimney. Then we had it all painted a New England barn red. It was a very comfortable home. Evan had a nice room to stay in on the weekends.

My consulting work was slacking off, so I took a job in Dover as organization trainer for the nonprofit New Hampshire Community Loan Fund. It was my job to address the economic inequality faced by homeowners in manufactured housing parks in New Hampshire. The landlord owned the park, and the tenants owned their homes and rented their lots from the landlord. The landlords were free to raise the rents and they did. The manufactured homes, although called trailers, could not easily be moved once seated on their lot. So, the landlord could raise the lot rents as high as he wanted, and the homeowners had to pay. The landlords were supposed to maintain good roads, water, and septic systems, but they often failed to provide these services effectively and the homeowners had no recourse for rent and utility problems.

It was my job to organize the owners of the manufactured houses into cooperatives. I would train the members of the park, teaching them how to elect a board of directors, set up committees, and use the parliamentary procedure in *Robert's Rules of Order*. Once organized, the cooperative would ask the Loan Fund for a loan large enough to buy the whole housing park from the landowner. After that the resident homeowners could run the park themselves. I provided ongoing coaching. I liked being able to help these groups of people come together and improve their situation.

I enjoyed talking about organization development and my successes with Parker, my boss at the Loan Fund whose father had run a well-known pizza parlor in Dover. On a few of my trips to train people at a co-op, I was accompanied by a colleague, Jane. She had big cheeks and darting brown eyes. Her job was essentially the same as mine, but she used a more confrontational style with the residents of the parks. She happened to live in one of the trailer parks. I didn't suspect she held a grudge against me. The Loan Fund and our small team were quite successful, establishing about twenty cooperative parks, all of which flourished.

I was very proud of this work, helping people learn more democratic and communication skills so they could improve their physical and mental lives.

8.

Increasing Devotion to the Course

In 2004 I attended the Miracles Alliance Fall Celebration for students of *A Course in Miracles* in a large gymnasium at the University of Hartford. I listened to several speakers I had heard before, and then David Hoffmeister was introduced as an impromptu speaker. He was tall, had a big shock of red hair, and his face was red as if he had spent too much time outside in the sun. I thought he looked like a beach bum from California, probably peddling some form of Scientology. But he spoke about how he was travelling around the country, going to *A Course in Miracles* meetings and talking about how to put the Course into practice in everyday life. The other speakers had been theoretical; this was different. When he finished speaking, he walked across the large room and sat next to me. I was a bit surprised.

"Hi, I'm David," he said and extended his hand.

"Hi, I'm Andy." I shook his hand. "Where did you say you started your trip?"

"In Cincinnati, at a little place I call the Peacehouse."

"Oh really, do you live there by yourself?"

"No, there are three of us, all focused on disseminating information about the Course. Other people drop by from time to time."

"Do you have a website?"

"Yes, I do. Just type in my name, David Hoffmeister."

When we talked briefly between speakers, I experienced him as genuine and at peace. After that I went to his web page and saw that many of his previous talks were transcribed. I read some of them in which David had simplified key Course points. For example, he wrote that "You are not a person with a mind. You are wholly, purely, completely Mind." This made perfect sense to me, after having read the twelve hundred pages of the Course several times. I went to hear him speak two more times in New England and began to follow his talks as they were published on his website. I was beginning to want to live the Course in a practical way and it seemed as though Hoffmeister was the only Course leader doing that. Later I interpreted his sitting next to me as the beginning of a special foreordained connection.

I would be applying Course lessons soon enough. A few days later, at the Loan Fund, my colleague, Jane, the one who lived in one of our trailer parks, approached me in my office late one afternoon when we were alone and said, "I've been telling lies about you to Parker." Parker was the vice president and our boss. At first, I was surprised and shocked.

She went on. "You use all this fancy organizational development jargon, and you have long talks with Parker in his office. I'm afraid you'll take over and I'll lose my job." She paused to hear my upset reaction. My first thought was to defend what I was doing. But by this time, I had been studying and applying the lessons of *A Course in Miracles* for many years. Lesson 135 concludes: "I will not defend myself, because the Son of God needs no defense against the truth of his reality." So, I told Jane that everything was okay and made no attempt to defend myself with her or with my boss. Although I noticed that, in the following weeks, he no longer invited me into his office to chat.

Then one day a few board members in one of the co-op trailer parks were trying to drum out one of their number, Hal, off the board. I defended Hal vigorously and some of them got mad at me. They must have made reports about me to Parker because he summarily fired me. I was surprised, as I really hadn't done anything wrong. Yet Jane's priming of Parker had led him to mistrust me.

Anyway, I held true to the Course and did not defend myself with either Jane or Parker. On the contrary, when I happened to bump into Jane later on the street, I gave her a big hug, thus practicing the core ACIM principle of forgiveness. As a symptom of how much I had brainwashed myself, I actually felt good about being fired. It gave me more time to devote to my study of the Course. I was determinedly hearing a different drummer. I casually assumed that the relatively high income Melissa earned was plenty to cover us.

I began to take a closer look at my relationship with Melissa relative to the Course. The Course says, "The special relationships of the world are destructive, selfish, and childishly egocentric. Yet, if given to the Holy Spirit, these relationships can become the holiest things on earth—the miracles that point the way to the return to heaven." I wanted to give our relationship to the Holy Spirit, to bring Melissa with me on my spiritual journey. Yet she had no interest in *A Course in Miracles* whatsoever. I remember putting a copy of the Course next to the bed. Melissa said, "Oh no, you are not bringing that in here." So, I read it in the other room. I was a bit disappointed.

I thought maybe I could bring her around indirectly, through a spirituality that was acceptable to her. Buddhism seemed to suit her. She agreed to join me on a weeklong Tibetan Buddhist meditation retreat in Boston, "The Pointing Out Way," with noted Buddhist teacher Dan Brown. The retreat was good, and I took lots of notes. During the final meditation I felt I had a period of transcendence in which my thinking stopped completely. Melissa tolerated the retreat okay but had no spiritual experience.

I attended weekly Course study groups in several towns in New Hampshire. In July 2008, I made this journal entry.

Riding back from the New London, NH ACIM group I noticed I was feeling very good, joyful, about my understanding of the Course and also my application of forgiveness. As fearful thoughts about the basement water leak or my unemployment came up today, I noticed them, reframed them as illusions seen through my false belief system, and let them go. Ultimately, the Course says, "There is no world." I completed my written Summary of ACIM, drawn largely from my David Hoffmeister binder and his audios. I feel I completely understand the metaphysics of the Course. I feel empowered to watch my thoughts and, if any are noticeably upsetting, change my mind about them. "I am blessed as the Son of God."

A year later, I wrote: "I have chosen to follow the Love branch of the road. All upset coming from fear-based beliefs need not be. I simply change my mind, ask Holy Spirit, and experience peace and joy."

After spending a year unemployed and studying *A Course in Miracles* full time, I took a job as the director of an adult day program for people with disabilities. I wanted to be of service and contribute the income to our household. This work went very well for a year and, although it was demanding, I enjoyed my interactions with the clients. But then as I was leaving work one day, one of my clients' parents called me.

"You're not a good director. You run a lousy program. Mainly, you're treating my son badly. Why you're... you're just a worm. That's what you are, a worm." She was slurring her words and was obviously very drunk.

I thanked her for her feedback, said her son was being well treated, and suggested we talk about it in the morning. I didn't feel a need to call the company president, as that would be defending myself. Evidently, she called the president, because he fired me, only to later find out that she had been lying. I saw this firing as still another opportunity for me to have the time to study the Course in more depth.

Looking back on it now, I can see how I was letting ideas from the Course lead me into self-destructive behavior. I had been fired from two jobs in a row because I hadn't defended myself or spoken up for myself. On a basic level this seemed stupid, but I saw these as opportunities to trust God's plan for me. Also, I was taking advantage of the fact that Melissa, as a clinical psychologist and an advanced registered nurse practitioner (ARNP), was making a lot of money.

I was falling more and more under the spell of David Hoffmeister. He said that he was "leading us out of the world," and he counseled followers to leave both property and people behind, as these distracted us from our focus on God.

In August 2008 I attended a retreat with David Hoffmeister in Kentucky. David could speak about the Course for long stretches of time without a break and my initial attempts to get a word in edgewise were met with no response, so I learned to be quiet and to just listen. David talked about special relationships. He said that we should play "fifty-two pickup" with our relationships. This meant handing all our relationships over to the Holy Spirit, i.e., ending them, and waiting for Him to perhaps deal them back to us in a different form. When I expressed my fear of sacrificing my relationship with Melissa, David said, "The Course was designed for relationships. There is no sacrifice," so, I could let my relationship worries go and the Holy Spirit would fix it all for me.

During a break, David came over and sat next to me. I was a bit surprised and pleased. He told me he wanted to develop "a core of polished professional materials, well made, so they can have wide distribution," perhaps with Gary Renard's endorsement. He then asked me if I would compile and edit his first book. Yay! I happily agreed. That invitation really invigorated me. Now I was definitely not only accepted but appreciated, seen as one who could help David promulgate his message.

When I got home, I began assiduously editing transcripts of David's talks into chapters for his book, which I titled *Awakening through A Course in Miracles*. In the chapter called "Come Join Us" David says: "We were brought together by God to serve the Plan of Awakening, to treat each other with dignity, respect, kindness, and holiness, and to Awaken to our Divine Love." This was exactly what

I was looking for. I wanted to do the good things with others and especially to awaken to the divine love that must be asleep inside me.

There were hundreds of pages of material. It was a big task in that these were transcripts of David's spoken words. Spoken language differs significantly from written language. All the "ahhs," "errs," "you knows," and "likes" had to be taken out and partial sentences cleared up. Questions from the audience needed to be boiled down to their essence. Some of the talks were quite complex. Each talk needed to be sequenced in a logical order that I conceived, and the whole thing needed to flow coherently in engaging prose. This involved deletion of thousands of unneeded words. I chose not to put my name on it as editor, but to humbly say it was edited by "volunteers."

After a few months of compiling and editing, it was in final form, and it was promptly published. It was a great book. In a sense, I owned the words and felt that I was on the inside now, and to a certain degree, I felt "chosen." Now I could begin to anticipate experiencing the miracles promised by David and the Course.

But I didn't see him or hear from him. Except for a brief thank you, David didn't even comment on all the work I had done putting the book together. Where I thought we might be beginning a partnership, there was only a brief mention of my editing on his end. I was disappointed, but I decided that it must be my role to work without any egoic appreciation needed on my part, to simply do God's will and the love and spiritual rewards would come later. I was used to a stern, critical paternal figure. I likewise made assumptions that God and his chosen one, David, had very high standards and that my efforts to date were headed in the right direction but not yet worthy of recognition.

While I was editing *Awakening*, Evan had gotten an IT job and an apartment in Manchester, so I only saw him on weekends. We would play racquetball, chess, or ride our bikes. Sometimes we had deep discussions of themes in *A Course in Miracles*.

Meanwhile, my wife Melissa was making jewelry and watching crime dramas on television in the basement. She had shown little interest in the book I had written and showed no interest in the book I was editing, a major disappointment for me. The Course says, "The special love relationship is the ego's most boasted gift." Could I, should I, maintain this relationship? The ego is the false self-identification I wanted to let go of. Apparently, my special love relationship was my biggest distraction away from God. I thought about this often.

Here is an example of how I was applying Course metaphysics to my life. I had been attending a monthly investment club meeting which I really enjoyed. One night I forgot to go. Bang, I woke up at four in the morning with the shock of remembering I'd missed it and I immediately felt heavy and stuck in guilt. How disrespectful that was! Then I thought, *Hey, I don't have to do this. I'm thinking about something in the past—a lie, no reality. There is only now. The guilt is about my imagined separation from God. I don't want to be separate. What's true now? I am fine. I am not a body; I am as God created me. Holy Spirit, help me see it differently. I feel the love of God within me now.* And then I felt free! Right away. It was so easy.

At a devotional retreat at Hoffmeister's Living Miracles Center in Utah in December 2008, we watched the quantum physics movie

What the Bleep. David often interpreted movies for us as the Holy Spirit guided him. In quantum physics, there isn't an "out there" out there. Matter is completely insubstantial, like thought. Our thoughts affect this "reality."

David related how: the brain doesn't know the difference between what it sees and what it remembers; the same neurons fire. This explains why we can experience different emotions watching a movie, even though we knew before we started watching that it was just a show. We chose to suspend disbelief and to be captured by the story. Outside the movie theater, we are captured by the world's story, and by our own, and we don't realize that our unconscious mind plays a part in it.

We choose our experience. Our unconscious mind prejudges, preselects what our inner programming believes. Our senses are bombarded by four hundred billion bits of data per second, so, we select only what we want. We match patterns that we know. This confirms our personal reality. We are basically on autopilot. With the ego in charge, we live in the chaos of the world. The ego is incompetent to choose at a higher level.

David and the Course therefore advocate, "Holy Spirit, decide for God for me" as a constant and practical prayer. David said this yielding to the Spirit offers immediate results.

I wanted to experience this guidance. I aspired to hear the voice of the Holy Spirit. I understood this need not necessarily be an actual voice in my head but could appear as my intuition or a hunch. I thought my ability to hear, or be aware of, the Holy Spirit's voice was just around the corner for me as I kept studying the Course.

Then I thought about Melissa and my relationship with her.

How does hearing the Holy Spirit relate to me and Melissa? The Course says that our special love relationships are of no value. On the contrary, they are egoic distractions intended to keep us from the love of God. This condemnation of the special love relationship was hard for me to accept because I loved Melissa and I loved my son, Evan. I felt love for my sister and her family too. I was an extraverted person, attached in close relationships with my friends. Yet the Course devotes nine chapters to undoing the special relationship.

And David took it one giant step further.

David said that Jesus had given him a guiding rule pertaining to our relationships— "no people pleasing." David wrote in a handout:

> People-pleasing is walking on eggshells in order to smooth things over with others (for example, family members or even a Course group) so as not to rock the boat. People pleasing is an ego mechanism which looks for love, recognition, and respect from others instead of from within.

Well, I thought, I don't walk on eggshells to please others, that wouldn't be good. I'm okay with looking within.

> Guilt always comes from holding onto the false self-concept and to past associations, both of which were made by the ego to keep you from soaring. These past associations may seem familiar and comfortable, but they always entail compromise and sacrifice. These beliefs must be exposed and released, for they cover over the Present in awareness.

I wanted to soar. My past associations included my family and friends. To expose and release them would involve moving away from them, say to the Living Miracles Center in Utah. And I was not yet ready to do that.

To undo people pleasing, speak from the heart, devoting yourself to the Course in attitude and perspective. And don't be concerned about other people's reactions as you have been in the past. The straightforward, direct approach may seem to make waves, but it is always the best. Otherwise, the denial and repression build, and you can feel as if you will explode. Some of your peers may seem to fall away, but many, many mighty companions will show up from every direction.

This was a call for a dramatic change. Yes, I was willing to lose my current group of friends if it meant I would gain many mighty companions. I assumed the mighty companions would include David and the Messengers.

People-pleasing is like a lot of false contracts that have been made to keep the illusion of love in place. When you let go of these contracts, you find enormous blessing—beyond what you could imagine.

The only literal contract I could think of was my marriage contract. So, if I let it go, would I experience "enormous blessing"? I began, hesitantly at first, to buy in to this idea of no people pleasing and to use it in my perception of Melissa and my communication with her. Melissa was an introvert. My implementation of "no people pleasing" resulted in significantly less empathic communication between us. I didn't have to please Melissa. My thinking was different; in a sense I was hardened. Sometimes I even thought of Melissa as an ego temptress I needed to resist.

This acceptance of no people pleasing slowly soaked into my mind, even though it was completely opposed to the main thesis of my *Creating Harmonious Relationships* book, which extolled compassionate communication, empathically listening to find the positive hopes in others, and proactively expressing love to others. In a sense, no people pleasing was opposite to who I was. Yet I wanted approval from David Hoffmeister, whom I was beginning to see as God's representative. He had never even mentioned my book, although I had sent him a copy. I took his words as the words of Jesus, which must be the truth. So, I stoically prepared myself for no people pleasing.

My thinking under the influence of *A Course in Miracles* proceeded to develop along these lines. My job is to listen to the Holy Spirit and follow guidance. I must avoid the ego part of myself, which indulges in "pride, pleasure, and attack." T-6.V-A Melissa is an image I have made. There is no meaning in form. I am not a person (of the ego thought system.) I am mind (of Christ/Holy Spirit). My purpose is forgiveness; seeing my false dreams, their underlying false beliefs, and letting them all go. All my ordering of thought is usurping God, an attack upon my Self. I know nothing. So, I open to the Holy Spirit and listen; then I speak honestly and openly.

In 2009 I hadn't worked in over a year. I went with Melissa to see our financial advisor. We walked into her suburban office and sat down. The adviser asked me cheerily if I was still looking for a job and I said "no" definitively. The adviser looked startled.

"Perhaps you're thinking of a new line of work?

"Nope. The only thing I want to do with my time is study *A Course In Miracles*."

They looked at each other. Both of them offered counterarguments, but to no avail. Melissa took this very hard.

"I feel betrayed," said Melissa. "This isn't what I signed up for. I'm frightened that we have no secure financial future planned out. And I hate this religious stuff, both the haughty way you say it and the impersonal content. I have no interest or belief in your spirit."

"Hold on a minute, honey," I said. But she was too worked up. As soon as we got home, she drove off to take the afternoon to herself. The next day she was better. We were again comfortable with each other, and I was grateful for that.

Publicly saying no to the world of employment was a significant step for me. I was no longer straddling that fence. It was a declaration that God was my goal. I felt more secure in my being able to spend time with Him now that Melissa "officially" understood my priority. I pointed out that she had only gained as I had become more loving, and she agreed. We also discussed this with her psychotherapist. Melissa said she hated religion that excluded discussion. I said that I was becoming aware that I was not so much religious as I was a mystic, seeking direct communion with God. I was, however, frustrated not being able to hear the voice of God.

One night I had a dream in which the vice president who had fired me told me, "I'm glad to have you around; I can always count on you." Ta-da! I was delighted by this sign that the forgiveness, which is so central to the Course, was working and growing in my mind!

In the spring I picked up David Hoffmeister at the airport in Manchester. He had come to attend a big Camp for Miracles event nearby and was staying at my house. As I pulled up at the arrivals, I noticed him immediately. He was the tallest person there and had a large paunch under a tight yellow polo shirt that bulged over his belt. His head was a big, bald. shiny oval. He wore baggy khaki shorts, white socks, and large tennis shoes. I had the flicker of a thought that he looked like a huge grown baby. He put his suitcase in back and slowly lowered himself into the passenger seat. As he did so the car leaned a little down to the right. After the smile and the *hi how are you, good trip* talk, we rode in silence back to my house. He had a calm, serene demeanor. I was ransacking my mind for something spiritual and intelligent to say but I couldn't think of anything.

Finally, I asked, "Is spiritual awakening really that good?"

"Yes!"

"Am I doing it right?" (I had shared with him on the phone about my Course study and meditations.)

"Yes, keep listening to the Holy Spirit."

I hoped he would add more. Was there a trick to hearing the Holy Spirit? But he didn't say any more. I was afraid to ask more for fear of appearing weak or losing his approval. We arrived at the Camp for Miracles which was taking place at a school with several buildings in a woodsy area. We set up the materials table, prominently displaying his new book *Awakening through A Course in Miracles*. During the sessions, I recorded David's talks, which were right in line with *A Course in Miracles*.

In the afternoon everyone lined up in two lines facing each other. While beautiful soft music played, the top person from one line would close his or her eyes and walk down between the lines. Those on both sides caressed him or her and whispered phrases like "Welcome, beloved" into their ears. When I went slowly down between the lines, I heard the gentle whispers and even more felt the caresses and smooth thighs of some of the women who pressed up against me. License for this intimacy was apparently granted by having the eyes closed and being part of a holy ritual.

Having completed the walk, the person would join the line at the bottom. This "Angel Walk" was wonderful! I felt so loved, so appreciated, like I was being escorted up the stairway to heaven by angels. It was absolutely my best experience yet. This wasn't reading or hearing about love. This was the lived, physical, sensual reality of love. And I wanted more of it.

In the evening after dinner there was a comedian, Jerry. He talked about how restaurants were trying to outdo themselves by bringing bigger and bigger pepper grinders to the table. The waiter would ask, "Would you like a little fresh pepper on that madam?" And Jerry acted out carrying in and grinding from a huge pepper shaker.

Jerry said he was in a restaurant the other day and ordered tea. The waiter asked if he wanted milk with it. Jerry said yes, and the waiter brought in a live cow and milked it next to the table. He acted it out brilliantly I thought Jerry was a riot. I looked over at David who had a bland smile on his face. I felt a bit sad for him, that he was separate from this worldly joy. *Would this happen to me too?* I thought with a twinge of fear.

That night, however, I had a guilty dream. I dreamed that a friend asked me to shoot someone for him because no one would suspect me. So, I did it, partially reasoning that there was no life in bodies. It turned out the victim was a presidential candidate. I was able to pass through security in a hallway without arousing suspicion. Then I woke up feeling terribly guilty about committing murder. I was very relieved to find that it was only a dream.

For over a year I had been going deeply into the Course and into my mind, apparently with no strong protest from my ego. I was pleased to have had this dream because I interpreted it to mean that my ego was beginning to feel the heat from my strengthening true self, and the ego was becoming more desperate in trying to make me feel guilty. With hindsight, I wonder if the candidate I killed represented the empathic self of my book.

One afternoon, I had a semi-mystical experience: I was meditating, and the thought popped into my mind that the thing that was holding me back was that I didn't want to give up control. So, I decided to give up control to the Holy Spirit and God. I saw a little light in my mind and instantly said yes; it got brighter, and I instantly said, "Yes, brighter, yes, wow, yes, peace, yes, joy, yes, yes, yes." It was like I was breaking through frames in a movie very quickly without knowing where I was or where I was going, just enjoying the ride. On and on. I am not Andy. I am Christ mind complete and healed and whole because that is real, a true idea.

Melissa had some legitimate complaints. I got a $100 ticket for running a stop sign and Melissa shouted at me: "I'm going to have to pay for that because you are no longer bringing home a paycheck!"

I forgave her, did one of David's spiritual worksheets to shift my thinking from a temporal focus to a spiritual focus on peace of mind. I also began carefully following all traffic laws. Melissa later apologized, explaining that she was worried what would happen to her if I lost my license. She acknowledged that I was a great help to her setting up the tent and displays for her at her jewelry shows.

One day Melissa sent an email to me from work, titled "Panic," about our financial situation. This time I didn't overreact. I realized it was about nothing real: my projection of false belief. In a calm state of mind, I sent her a reply that all of our needs were met. Apparently soon after going to sleep, I was so restless in bed that Melissa had to leave and go sleep downstairs. I think I was tossing in restless dreams all night, triggered by thoughts of radically shifting my relationship with Melissa.

In the kitchen the next morning, she lowered her eyebrows and asked, "If I died, would you sell the house and move to David's community in Utah?"

"Probably, I replied matter-of-factly. Whatever the Holy Spirit tells me to do. Right now, that's to not have a job and study the Course,"

"And what does your Source think about *me* and my financial concerns?" There was a tremor n her voice.

"God loves you; all your needs are met and will continue to be met."

"I'm feeling guilty about spending anything."

"There isn't a problem. You are fine just as you are."

I had been feeling that I was Spirit for extended parts of the day, and I loved it; just a vast, peaceful feeling. I took my time, laughed at mistakes. I asked the Holy Spirit for help with Melissa's financial distress. In November 2009 I got a call from a guy in Pennsylvania saying I might get a big sum of money in the future from the sale of some old gas leases my mother had. This made both of us very happy!

Not long after that the phone rang. It was a well-known Course teacher calling to thank me for sending her David's book that I had edited. She loved it, felt opened and touched by it, found it deeply helpful. She said that the book said what she wanted to say better than she could say it. She invited me to come anytime to her regular ACIM meeting in Boston and stay over. I felt great about this.

One night in December I experienced some disturbance in my visual field. It was like the lenses of my glasses were floating around and sometimes would blank out or go off the screen entirely and I couldn't see. Then I felt very sick, feverish, and wiped out. I collapsed and covered my head on the couch, convinced I had caught a nasty flu. I tried telling myself that I was Spirit, and that sickness was not possible, but it wasn't working. So, I put more genuine desire into my mind. The Course tells us that we become sick only as the result of our own (unconscious) decision. I told myself that I reversed my decision to be sick because I had no need of it. I repeated, "I have no desire to be a separate, weak body when I am actually Spirit. I am God's Son, complete and healed and whole."

Then I seemed to be given a hint: that by lying down I was demonstrating to the universe that I really was sick. The Course says that I learn by teaching, and I teach by demonstrating. So, I got up and demonstrated my health by going out and shoveling the snow off the driveway. While shoveling I told myself: "I am not weak, but strong; There is nothing my holiness cannot do; God's will for me is perfect happiness; I accept God's will for happiness for me; God's will is wholly without opposite; I am sustained by the love of God; I want the peace of God." And, lo and behold, all my symptoms disappeared! I felt great! The driveway was cleared of snow, and I was filled with gratitude for this mini miracle. Even Melissa was impressed. I became even more committed to the spiritual path.

During football season I noticed I was having an emotional reaction to a Patriots football game on TV. The Patriots were behind, and Tom Brady threw a long pass to a receiver who caught it in the end zone, putting them ahead. I let out a big "Yeah!"

Then I caught myself. How absurd. A TV was just some changing colors and sounds, completely meaningless. I gave it all the meaning it had for me; I could tell I had judged it because I had an emotional reaction. From meaningless sense impressions, I perceived form and meaning. I made up an interpretation about people and gave meaning where nothing real happened. Nothing happens in nothing. I am not a person, but I have been hallucinating the life of a person. Viewed from within the separation, nothing happens except that I delay my awakening. I then accepted that what I thought I saw was false and withdrew any value I had put on it. It had no power to affect me; I felt no emotional charge. I let it go.

I wrote in my journal:

But now I am wondering what to do next. What was true of the football game must be equally true of my wife, Melissa. I feel detached. I do not know anything. I am God's Son. I ask the Holy Spirit in me to "Help me see it differently." I am worthy of miracles; help me see a miracle. Replace my false images. God's Will for me is perfect happiness, I accept His Will for me, and His Will is wholly without opposite.

During my meditation one morning in March, I had the experience of being one with God! After some initial settling in, I came to focus on the idea, "I am His holy sinlessness Itself." I thought, *Since this is the truth, and there is no sin, it is impossible for me to have separated from God. Therefore, right now, I am still one with God and all of creation.*

Everything then shifted and brightened. I felt completely wonderful, joyful, and relaxed; my mind was alert and free throughout. Mostly I experienced the oneness of my self and God and all of creation. I noticed that God had no form. I was completely content. I felt an impulse to share the experience and blessed the people who came to mind. I had the impression of vertical white light coming down. I didn't want it to end, but eventually I had the sensation of being gradually lowered into my body again. After this I had a delightful interaction with Melissa over breakfast that brought us even closer together.

A week later I began studying David's online Spiritual Mind Training program. It counseled, "Watch your mind to see what seems to stir up feelings of guilt and fear, observe what your mind attaches the guilt and fear to, and welcome the experience of innocence as you turn to the Holy Spirit for guidance." I had read about the guidance others received and thought to myself, *Well, I don't receive such obvious indications of God's will for me, but I'll just plod along like a good doo-bee (who unfortunately happens to not quite be worthy of God's notice).* Although I had gotten all sorts of rein-forcement during meditation, I still felt I needed to see some sign or symbolism in the world (or else perhaps I was just fooling myself in meditation).

Shortly thereafter, I received blindingly obvious guidance. First, I got an email from David inviting me to come to a summer retreat. Then, I got a call from Ben, a close friend of David's, saying he'd like to put on a movie gathering at my house.

I said, "Are you sure? I live in the sticks. Wouldn't Boston be better?"

Ben said, "I asked Spirit, and your name came up very clearly."

So, Ben came and led an ACIM gathering at my house. I had in-vited three of my old Course friends whom I'd let drift away, but now we all had a good time together and were reconciled.

Ben also had a lengthy, positive communication with my wife, Melissa. Previously she had not wanted me to go to Course events. That night I showed her a list of ACIM retreats I could possibly at-tend. She took one look at the list and said definitively, "Go to the one from May 28 to June 4."

I said, "But that's a full week, and it's in Utah."

She said, "That's okay. I'm going to Austin that week to see my parents."

So, I searched for airline tickets and there was *one* cheap fare left. I called Sophia, the Messenger coordinator, and there was only *one* place left for the retreat. At this point I felt I had internalized the Voice for God, "I'll take it!"

In the movie we saw at the gathering at my house, *Evan Al-mighty,* God resorts to dropping lumber and bird shit on Evan to get

99

him to take the hint. Even the movie was the Holy Spirit's guidance for me. Now I saw that my guidance needed to escalate to almost the same dramatic level before I could see it and accept it for what it was. I had tried to shift Ben off target. I had given my wife the opportunity to deny me my extended retreat. But I thanked God that my ego attempts to prove my unworthiness failed. I felt blessed. It could only be that I am innocent and worthy, as God created me. I prayed: *Holy Spirit, I am willing to follow Your guidance, and I desire to seek it and accept it at all times and in all matters. Thank you. Amen.*

In April, a Messenger called me from Utah and suggested that Leila be my mentor in the Living Miracles Training Program. I was angry and disappointed because Leila didn't rank in the hierarchy at the Utah community. Her speaking and accent revealed that she had had less higher education. Helen suggested I use David's Levels of Mind instrument, which I did. And I saw I was valuing the following beliefs more than the peace of God: 1) People need to be smart intellectually and know a lot to be valuable as mentors. 2) I am better than people who don't know the ACIM book as well as I do. 3) Martha and the Messengers don't think much of me; I deserve a better mentor.

I wrote:

Yech, I don't want those judgmental thoughts at all; what a cheap identity. I would much rather have the Peace of God. This morning I read Leila's very honest blog messages and decided I liked her. I called her, we had a wonderful conversation and now I have a mentor! The next day I had another beautiful joining with Leila:

so much happiness, joy, love, peace, gratitude, ease. Like the movie *Brother Sun, Sister Moon*, or the 23rd Psalm. It feels very, very, good.

In a meditation in May, I experienced two hours of perfect happiness with God while sitting on the burgundy living room couch. It was a period of grace. Everything was effervescent and happy. It was very much like falling totally in love, but with no person. Just being in love; heightened senses, everything in the universe is fine, experiencing a kind of cool delightful glow through my core. I was very alert and very at ease, talking with God, feeling His love for me, and telling Him of my love for Him. "Father, I love You." "I want only this." I felt completely free, like I couldn't do anything wrong. Finally, the effervescence began to settle down and I again felt as if I were very slowly parachuting back down into my body. It was a sustained miracle. I was reading Rumi's poetry the day before and loving it. I felt like I would be delighted to be a slave of God, for this God only gives and never coerces; His will is my will.

9.

Three Pivotal Retreats

I attended a three-week Messengers Retreat that summer at Living Miracles Center in Utah. David's twelve "Messengers" had completely devoted themselves to David and to living *A Course in Miracles*. They had given all their money to Living Miracles. All of them but two were women.

The location of the Center in Strawberry River Canyon is stunning. Just like the Holy Land, a desert, with a river cutting between steep canyon walls and scattered sagebrush. I could smell the sun-baked earth. One morning I followed an abandoned mine into what I imagined to be an ascetic monk's cave.

During the retreat we had some great laughs and did a trust walk in which one participant would lead a blindfolded participant through the sagebrush and the rocky ground. With patience and physical cues, I was able to get Willow, a fellow student, to step down off a small flat rock. Afterward, Willow, who was Native American from Montana, said she could really trust me.

David gave a talk to about sixteen of us in the lodge living room. I was leaning on some pillows on the floor. He said that the separation from God was the "psychotic break." We should let the world of illusion collapse and return to sanity. Listen and follow. The next morning, I went to the kitchen, sat, a bit unsure of myself, waited, and then after a while was surrounded by pretty women reading mystical poetry aloud!

Silent Monday—I wrote:

I am a living miracle. I am the end I seek. I am Love loving. I listen to the Voice for God instant by instant, that I may think and do His Will. God's Will for me is perfect happiness, and I am perfectly happy trusting and following Him. My heart is filled with gratitude and appreciation for my brothers and sisters who joyfully carry me along.

In a group session Tuesday morning, Olivia, a very tall blond Messenger, offered to "link up" with me to help remind me when I was distracted away from following Holy Spirit. I was so happy about this! I now had a real mighty companion! She chose me for her group. Olivia would also be at the upcoming retreat in Majorca! In the evening, we all sat around a campfire singing Beatles songs as Jeff, one of the volunteers, accompanied us on the guitar. There was a gorgeous sunset.

Thursday in the group, Sandy, a participant, said, "I can feel your tender, loving presence." (Wow! Healing!)

Willow said, "I was so touched by what you said about spirit; it meant so much to me." After watching the movie, *It's Complicated*, I roasted the special relationship, that is, I pointed out how impossible it would be to turn any of the relationships of the actors into holy relationships.

Then we paired up on facing chairs and practiced, one-on-one, looking deeply into each other's eyes. This was called eye-gazing. My experience was of loving recognition. I became aware of how much I had really been longing to experience the love of God, to come fully into my identity as the Son of God. I thought this awareness was stirred to life in me by the steady eye-gazing of Messengers Olivia, Charlotte, and Helena, which felt like joining, acceptance, and blessing at a spirit level. The guidance was: pause, listen, and follow. As we drove out of the canyon, I saw a mountain goat with curving horns calmly looking down at us, which I interpreted as a positive sign that my whole spiritual endeavor was meant to be.

Back in New England, I had an experience of combining my consulting work with my spiritual inclination. I was sought out by Daniel Stein, a former client, who wanted me to help his community integrate their new rabbi. We met in the morning in a side room of the magnificent synagogue. Daniel was very positive about how I had helped him previously and certain that I was the consultant he wanted. I had some anxiety thinking about it. Then I decided to turn it over to God and to ask for His guidance every step of the way. This felt good. In the afternoon I spoke with the executive board of the synagogue. They said their new scholarly rabbi was at odds with the staff and the board, and they asked me to help. The rabbi had appointed an assistant without letting the board engage in the usual review process. Then the two of them had made a series of decisions without involving the board.

I met with the rabbi, who was probably in his early thirties, on Tuesday. We talked and I listened to him empathically, gaining his trust. When I met with him again on Friday, however, he was discouraged. The president, an older man in his sixties, had just told the rabbi that he would be fired at the end of his contract, one year from now. I asked the rabbi to tell me about his mission, what he really wanted. His mission turned out to be sharing the love of God with the congregants, including the staff and the board. He acknowledged having been frightened by some previous board actions, after which he had become defensive and isolated. I told him he could turn that around if he wanted and I would help him, even if this turned out to be his last year. He said he would like to do that. So, we talked deeply about fear, love, and God.

Then we talked about what it might take on his part to shift the board and staff from viewing him with fear to viewing him with love. At the end of our meeting, he summarized his action plan: He would admit his initial fears and consequent mistakes. He would enthusiastically express his love for God, the congregants, and his mission. And he would commit to learning and practicing new communication skills.

When I left him, he was enthusiastic about what he would say at that night's executive and board meetings, putting it in his own words and those of the Torah. He expressed his gratitude to me and said he thought I would be great at his kind of work, for which I thanked him.

The next week, I met with the executive director of the synagogue. I listened to his lawyerly complaints about the rabbi until he was sure that I understood him. I pointed out that he had believed that the rabbi had intended to attack him personally and held on to that belief, even though he had learned subsequently that that had not been the rabbi's intention.

The executive director said that he himself could become aggressive in an argument and sometimes blew up. I told him this was his problem to fix, and that announcing it did not give him license to do it. He asked if I could help him. I said yes and told him to take a few slow deep breaths with me. He did so, noticed the calming effect, and was impressed. I told him it was the best way to interrupt the fight-or-flight response, to tell his brain he wasn't about to be killed. His eyes brightened and he sincerely thanked me. We both felt happy as we parted.

When I got home, I Skyped Leila, my mentor. I told her about the events and relaxed into a warm glow. Then I noticed a fearful thought arising in my mind, "What if my intervention at the synagogue doesn't work? What if they don't all join in harmony? Am I a phony?" Under her loving gaze, I looked at those thoughts and saw them as ego attempts to explain away the miracle. The miracle is now, in the moment, in the mind, and it is real. I cannot change the world and that is not my goal. It is to see it through the Holy Spirit's lens, and to respond to calls for love with love. The Holy Spirit brings the miracle. Leila stayed in loving connection with me until all my doubts had dissolved and my joy was constant again. I was so grateful for her joining with me.

June 27, 2010, journal entry I wrote with the sun streaming in the window:

Today I sat on the couch with my legs crossed, put a pillow behind my back, closed my eyes and began to meditate. And Christ called to me! I heard His Call and accepted, choosing to take my place among the saviors of the world. Christ showed me, at a feeling level, that I am Love, and I experienced that it was true. Hearing this Call so clearly this morning was powerful and uplifting. And

I am grateful to have finally heard it and accepted it. Since the Messengers Retreat, it seems I've become ready. It must have been the strength of Christ in me as I was coaching the Rabbi on his interpersonal communication.

I shared my experience of hearing and accepting the call with Melissa. She received it happily and confirmed that, during our decade together, I had done a complete turnaround from being fearfully defensive to being lovingly accepting. I spoke on the phone with Olivia, and she said now that I have accepted the call, I need to watch how I use my valuable mind. It is not helpful to compromise by seeking to fit in with people who do not understand.

In July, I was on Monhegan Island for a week with Melissa and four other couples. Monhegan is a beautiful place, with the ocean lapping all around, some seaweed washed up on the sandy beach, our rustic rented house with gray weathered shingles. There were also trails through Cathedral Woods, where people had built little fairy villages out of sticks, bark, and shells.

On Monday, I felt inspired to finish my compilation of David's video summaries on my laptop and gave it all my attention. That evening, however, Melissa expressed upset that I wasn't participating with her and the others. I also overheard a whispered remark, "Some spiritual people think they are better than other people," and felt guilty. I had violated expected husband and group-member roles.

So, poof, I compromised. The next day I stayed with them all day and washed plenty of dishes. My deliberate people-pleasing put the social climate back in balance.

But I felt guilty. I had put myself in that situation, felt pressured, and chosen for the ego. I had accepted an ego role and compromised my spiritual identity. I was glad no one from the Living Miracles community was there to see me. I resolved to spend a silent hermitage week alone in August. This idea was nixed by Melissa.

On July 25 we watched the movie *Inception* at home. It is a powerful allegory about the Son of God, in which Leonardo DiCaprio kills his wife. I wrote a summary of it, which Melissa read. She said, "You aren't going to shoot *me*, are you?" Metaphorically, she had some reason to fear. I wasn't going to shoot her, but the life of our relationship was growing weaker.

This was my "progress report" to Leila regarding the person/body-related things I had "undone" and given over to God/Holy Spirit. No more going to work. No more improving the house and yard. No more mountain biking. No more TV, reading fiction, history, or anything nonspiritual. I would, however, devote two hours each morning to prayer and meditation, which I loved.

Could I be stuck simply because I still lived with my wife? The Course says that changes in external circumstances are always helpful and that the special love relationship is the ego's most boasted gift, and one which has the most appeal to those unwilling to relinquish guilt. The Holy Spirit in the Course seems to be telling me that a marriage relationship is valueless and to let it go by moving out. And to do this I need a great deal of trust. Trust is necessary because I must remove this ego-cherished block before I can realize that letting it go is no sacrifice and feel a gift bestowed on me instead. But I'm not ready to do it now. I expect I can become clearer on this in Majorca, at the six-week retreat with David in the fall.

That evening I pulled a folder from the recycled folder pile and an ACIM card fell out of it: "Beyond this world is a world I want. I choose to see that world instead of this, for here is nothing that I really want." It was total, hit-the-nail-on-the-head confirmation. Yee haw! But it was about leaving this world as valueless. Jesus of the Bible wouldn't say the world was valueless. What about love?

I looked up the words of Jesus in the Bible; "Teacher, which is the greatest commandment in the Law?" Jesus replied: "'Love the Lord your God with all your heart and with all your soul and with all your mind.' This is the first and greatest commandment. And the second is like it: 'Love your neighbor as yourself.' All the Law and the Prophets hang on these two commandments." Matthew 22:36-40 This is what I want: to love God *and* other people. I pushed the dissonance between "love your neighbor" and the Course's condemnation of special relationships off into a corner of my mind, thinking this conflict would somehow reconcile later on.

I particularly noticed the benefit of focusing on "God is with me," as I met with Melissa to attempt to gain her agreement with the financial plan I had made. We got all the thoughts and feelings out. I was gentle; she agreed with the plan, and we had a long and loving hug. It is wonderful to have God with me all the time. First, we went to our financial planner, who asked me skeptically, "Are you really sure you want to do this?"

Then Melissa and I went to the lawyer and drafted the trust documents that would divide our money into thirds: one for her, one for Evan, one for a new foundation I was planning to set up to support spiritual endeavors. I still thought I was going to inherit a bunch of money. The plan I was given was being carried out.

I found a challenging situation in the Spiritual Mind Training Program: *How do you feel having watched the movie, The Butterfly Effect?* One scene vividly reminded me of visiting my brother Tony in the mental hospital with a guard present. I caught myself fearfully identifying as a person who had mental illness in his family. I stopped and reminded myself, *This is a fictional story. Nothing real is happening. The figures in the movie, and the figure watching them (Andy), are all unreal and nothing unreal exists. I need not have empathy for a symbol of weakness and victimization. I am not a person. I am God's Son, always perfectly safe.*

It was helpful to watch this movie because my emotional reaction showed me that I still believed in the illusion. Then I stopped and remembered that it was not real. It was all a dream. Whew. I asked the Holy Spirit to see it differently, and I let it go.

Prior to my departure for the Majorca retreat with David Hoffmeister, Melissa said to me, "I experience dissonance because your experience of 'God' involves separation from those you hold dear. God seems like a river that divides the world into believers and non-believers. Religions do that." Her sister had gone into a religious sect that separated them. I said that need not be so. (Although I wondered if it might indeed be so.)

In the fall of 2010, I participated in a six-week intensive devotional retreat hosted by David Hoffmeister and his Messengers on the island of Majorca in the Mediterranean off the coast of Barcelona, Spain. Participants came from all over the world. The setting of the big villa on the island was idyllic. Mandarin oranges grew on the property; the food was delicious. The climate was springlike, with the palm fronds moving slightly in the breeze.

David's select associates, the Messengers, were warm and loving to us over the entire six weeks. Again, we did an Angel Walk. One at a time each of us walked with eyes closed, gently guided along between two rows of people while loving words were whispered in our ears. We were caressed and even kissed on both sides. I felt extremely happy being the object of such warm affection and I also enjoyed giving it to others as they walked down between the lines.

On the second day of the Majorca retreat we gathered in a large living room on comfortable chairs or pillows on the floor. David sat in an armchair facing us. He exuded a calm presence; his voice was low and measured. The content of David's lectures was sublime. He talked about the metaphysics of the Course in such a way that it seemed like the God-given truth. At one point David said, "It is a metaphysical error to see causation in events, in form." I saw a crinkle of confusion on the face of a participant and thought I could clarify the point for him.

So, I spoke up and added, "Metaphysics refers to that which is beyond the physical, that which is at the level of mind or spirit. Spirit/mind is the true cause behind apparent causality in form."

Dead silence. At first, I was surprised. Then I began to feel anxious and embarrassed. I thought, *David, anyone, please say something*! Still nothing. I looked around at the twenty or so blank faces. A small agonizing eternity passed. Finally, David continued speaking as if I hadn't said anything. This showed me that my contribution was considered to be of no value whatsoever. David and the Messengers clearly had a monopoly on hearing the voice of the Holy Spirit and I was not among them. I saw that it was inappropriate for me to volunteer my thoughts. I felt lousy. Maybe David didn't value me as much as I thought.

About a week into the retreat, I was feeling that I wasn't really making spiritual progress. I wanted more. I told a few Messengers that I wanted to go deeper. We had a meeting, and it was arranged that I have an "assignment" with Olivia, the tall, blond Swedish Messenger. I was pleased to be put in an assignment with her and I was put in her discussion group.

The second day our discussion group met it was apparent that Olivia was not fully present but seemed to be in a sort of spiritual trance. She said in a soft voice something about not being there and that she couldn't lead the discussion group today. We all chose to remain with her. We lay in silence on a bunch of mats and pillows in a contiguous pile.

After a few minutes I felt miraculously lifted into a euphoric state. I was floating in the room, aware of all the vivid colors and complexities of the pillows and my comrades. I felt a peaceful, limitless joy! A gentle breeze flowed through the room. I had never experienced such a blissful state and would gladly have stayed there forever.

After what seemed like a long time, we slowly got up and meandered into the kitchen to eat. Still high, we began preparing sandwiches of roasted vegetables and cheese. From the side, a loving participant kissed me on the cheek and ear; I raised my arms in gratitude toward heaven. This movement happened to knock the sandwich off of Olivia's plate onto the floor. Red and yellow peppers on the tile floor. This broke the spell, as Olivia's face went suddenly red with anger at me. My mood crashed completely. Olivia glared at me with her large eyes; her head looked like a praying mantis. The participants wandered apart, awed by our recent mystical experience, and disoriented by its clipped conclusion.

A basic structure of the retreat included movies and breakout discussion groups of five or six people. As I mentioned, I was in the group headed by Olivia. The discussion was about the movie, *The Butterfly Effect*, and I had a lot I wanted to say. I saw amazing parallels between the movie and my life. I raised my hand, but Olivia didn't call on me. As the discussion went on, I raised my hand. Olivia glanced at me briefly, shifted her gaze, and called on someone else. I tried again. And again. I got angry. She was supposed to be in an assignment with me! After this frustrating experience, Olivia met me outside. Before I could say anything, she said, "Do you want to go shopping with me?"

I didn't want to go but figured that since she was my assigned Messenger I should go along. I drove her into town in one of the rental cars. She announced that she wanted to get a beanbag chair for the main room. I didn't think a beanbag chair was needed or even appropriate, but she said another Messenger would like it. She told me exactly which right and left to take until we stopped in front of a furniture store. We went in and there were no beanbag chairs on display. This didn't faze Olivia and she walked into a back room and, to my amazement, found a beanbag chair. She asked the manager about the chair, and he said it was defective and could be purchased at a discount. Olivia said we would buy it, then she clarified that *I* would buy it.

I thought this was like a Sufi teaching/learning opportunity for me to demonstrate that I was no longer hoarding personal money for my ego. So, we sat down to pay for it, but I didn't have enough Euros, so Olivia paid for it with her Messenger credit card on condition that I pay her back. When we got back to the villa, she said she wanted the money right away. I said it was late Saturday afternoon and the banks were closed, that I would give her the money on Monday after I had been to the bank. But she came by again Saturday evening asking for the money, and again on Sunday. This irrational behavior bothered me, and I explained again why I didn't have the money yet.

I was resentful and wanted to talk to David about Olivia. First, I found a Messenger and told her I wanted to talk to David, that it was about my assignment. The Messenger disappeared into the other end of the building and reported back shortly. David was available in his office, and she led me to it. I knocked.

"Come in."

I opened the door and stepped in. His office was fairly large, with a pattern of blue, green and white tiles around the walls; a broad ocean view, a couch with a red, yellow, and orange paisley pattern and a large wooden desk with a laptop, at which David was seated in a swivel chair. He turned to me and said, "Hi, Andy, I understand you want to talk to me."

"Yes," and I explained Olivia's strange behavior.

David looked at me for a moment; then he said, "You should have listened to your feeling of not wanting to go on that shopping trip with her." Then he turned in his chair and apparently returned to responding to emails.

That was all? I was dismissed? I stepped out and closed the door. I was pissed. In spite of all her crazy behavior, he was saying it was *my* fault! She was acting irrationally, and I guess he didn't want to hear about it. I felt alone with it.

I went and talked with Joyce, a sort of Messenger-in-training and group leader. She was very attractive and in a "teacher/learner" relationship with David, which included staying in his bedroom. Joyce sang beautifully, accompanied herself on the guitar and sometimes invited us to join in singing. Joyce invited me to join her discussion group, which I did.

In Joyce's small group I raged about Olivia for not letting me speak and for repeatedly demanding that I give her money for the beanbag chair. I beat up a pillow pretending it was her. Other participants confided in me that Olivia had shown peculiar behavior around relationships with them. She had lain down next to one of the gay participants and moved as if she wanted to have sex with him. He was shocked. Anyhow, my rollercoaster assignment with Olivia was over for good, or so I thought.

Over the weeks of the Majorca program, I developed a close friendship with Mexican participant Maria Hernandez, who was short and extremely pretty. Whenever she saw me, she would call out "Andy," raise her arms and give me a big hug. Wow, I loved that! Maria and I also had lengthy conversations about life, David's teachings, and ACIM. She was in the process of divorcing her husband, selling her house in Australia, and was contemplating giving all her money to Living Miracles. She was well ahead of me.

Halfway through the retreat, a very attractive Irish woman, Fiona, arrived. She said a Messenger had told her she was to complete an assignment with me. I was thrilled. An assignment meant that, where the Holy Spirit and the Messengers deemed it appropriate, two people would enter into a relationship for their mutual spiritual benefit. Fiona had green eyes and a mass of reddish curly hair like an afro, yet her skin was very fair Irish skin. I was delighted and we quickly became friends. On the second night after her arrival, we talked late into the evening and closed with a big hug. I noticed that I was beginning to get aroused and mentioned it. She pulled away and said that she was married. Okay, that simplified it; the relationship was to be platonic. Yet, I was pleased to be chosen and she became a good friend. We often held hands during the movies.

David's talks were consistent with the truth of *A Course in Miracles*. We watched an engaging movie every evening and then David interpreted it for us, showing us how the movie illustrated key metaphysical points of ACIM. It was the Holy Spirit who told David these interpretations. I was profoundly impressed and, despite a few blips, felt happy and secure within this metaphysical and apparently loving framework. It all also flowed seamlessly with the book of David's talks I had edited for him, *Awakening through A Course in Miracles*. One of the participants told me that it was that book that inspired her to come to this retreat. I loved it!

David's talks were all videotaped and a Messenger taught me how to edit the videos for publication on David's YouTube channel. After that I became a specialist in making and uploading videos. All this time the Messengers were encouraging people to sever their connections with home and to join the community. One day, as Maria Hernandez and I were lying by the pool Maria talked with me about the process of divorcing her husband. She was very determined to accomplish this efficiently and barely touched on his pained reactions.

There is a section of the Course (ACIM, T-14.IV.6:1-7) that says, "When you have learned how to decide with God, all decisions become as easy and as right as breathing. There is no effort, and you will be led as gently as if you were being carried down a quiet path in summer. Only your own volition seems to make deciding hard. The Holy Spirit will not delay in answering your every question what to do. He knows. And He will tell you, and then do it for you. You who are tired will find this is more restful than sleep."

The Messengers made several beautiful music videos, one of which repeated the idea from the Course "Decide for me." I was continually trying to have the Holy Spirit decide for me.

I experienced more Angel Walks as new groups of participants arrived. I felt extremely happy being the object of such warm affection and I also enjoyed giving it to others as they walked down between the lines. There were other times in which two or more people at the retreat would engage in intimate, but not necessarily sexual cuddling and touching. We coined the term "affectionating" for these experiences. I became friends with a woman from Georgia who had a great sense of humor.

I participated at 100 percent level during all the movie sessions, workshops, discussion groups, etc., for the entire six weeks. I was flying high at the end. We concluded the retreat with closing statements by each participant and the receiving of feedback, all of which was videotaped.

When my turn came, I was excited. I said a few nice things about the retreat and then I said that what I really wanted to focus on was "affectionating" and that I would give an example of it right there. I got up and laid across the laps of three pretty women. Everyone started to laugh. From this position I exchanged several comments with the other participants. I received a lot of positive feedback from participants and Messengers. Then my roommate offered me some feedback. There is a line in the Course which says, "Your part is only to offer Him a 'little willingness' to let Him remove all fear and hatred, and to be forgiven." (ACIM, T-18.V.2:5) Then, referring to my willingness to participate, "Andy has the biggest little willingness that I've ever seen."

I raised my head from the ladies' laps and said, "Oh, is that because we live in the same bunk, and you've had a look?" People immediately caught the idea that he had observed me changing clothes and that my member was the biggest "little willingness" he'd ever seen. Everyone was convulsed in laughter. I was on top of the world.

When I had made my flight reservations, I had left two extra days at the end in case I needed them. Well, I didn't need them. Everyone else left and I went and stayed in a little hotel in Alaior.

It was an attractive town, but there was a period of several hours when, compared with the retreat, the world seemed dry and boring. It felt like suddenly nobody spoke my language and there was no support for my way of life. I missed Maria and Joyce, two of the people I had found it easy to talk to. Joyce had decided she didn't want to be a Messenger and had flown back to California. Apparently, she wasn't willing to give up all of her worldly assets to David.

For months after my return to the United States I felt wonderful, that I was Spirit, not a body. The first day and night after I got back, I spent communicating with Melissa. I told her all about the retreat and she was happy for me. I wanted to join with God sooner, so I applied to be a volunteer at Living Miracles Center in Utah. I told Melissa and asked her to read this letter.

> I love you very much. I promised to always love you and it is true. And I feel a strong desire to follow God's will for me. These two do not conflict as I understand them. There can never be a conflict between God's will for me and my loving you. God is my primary goal and I need to follow Him. But sometimes I think that, if I go where I am guided, you will think I'm letting you down. So, I am caught in an uncomfortable place. I am not "leaving" you. My body may change location for a period of time, but love is a mental state. In our love for each other, we need to allow the other the freedom to fulfill their life's goals. We put this Khalil Gibran quote from *The Prophet* (1923) up in our bedroom:

> *But let there be spaces in your togetherness,*
> *And let the winds of the heavens dance between you.*
> *Love one another but make not a bond of love.*
> *Let it rather be a moving sea between the shores of your souls.*

I wrote in the letter: "I free you to follow your path. Will you free me to follow my path? You are my best and closest friend. I love you. I want you to be happy. Please don't set it up that if I follow God, you think I'm leaving you. That isn't true."

"This doesn't work for me," said Melissa with a hard edge. "You're planning to pick up and move to Utah. That's leaving me.

And I don't have another path to follow." She was both angry and pleading.

"But I do still love you," I said, my eyes beginning to sting. "God will make it okay. I don't know exactly how."

Melissa started to cry, and I hugged her until we both stopped crying.

It turned out that winter, that I wouldn't be getting the million-plus dollars I was expecting from gas leases, and Melissa would have to continue working full time. What upset me was that I thought the money coming was a sign from God because that possibility emerged right after I prayed for Melissa's relief. Actually, money never did sound like something God would deliver.

I saw my thinking as similar to Joan of Arc's thinking that God was on her side in the movie *The Messenger*. Joan saw a sword stuck in a field and interpreted it as a sign that God wanted her to go to war. But there are many unholy reasons why a sword might be stuck in a field. The Course says God/Spirit doesn't intervene in the world. A miracle is a shift in perspective, a time collapse. So, I was back to feeling clueless.

One cloudy morning in February, I drove into Manchester to get Evan out of jail for driving under the influence. The jail was a huge cement building with only slits for windows. I stated my purpose to a woman sitting behind a plexiglass barrier and then went through security, where they thoroughly checked me for any weapons or substances. I expected that he would be released promptly.

Unfortunately, the inmates had been given control over the discharge process, and they must have enjoyed stretching it out. I sat in one of the plastic chairs, which were arranged in rows under the fluorescent light bulbs and watched people come and go for hours. I didn't enjoy having no control over the situation. I felt like an ego prisoner unless I was meditating and being with Spirit.

Upon release, Evan was shaking and really liked my hugs. I told him I would always love him, and he said, "I love you too, Dad," and teared up a little. At his request, I drove him to his not-so-great double decker apartment. We promised to stay in close touch, but I felt sad leaving him off there, adult that he was.

I saw the movie *Danny Deckchair* with Melissa. Danny was a cement worker who broke loose from conventional Sydney society by going up in a hot air balloon. He crash-landed may miles away in the town of Macadamia, where he had a hilarious time being a new man and raising everyone's spirits. When dragged back to Sydney, he broke up with his partner because they shared different values. She asked, "What happened to you up there?" He replied, "Everything." I felt the same way having come back from Majorca. I was transformed and couldn't go back to being the way I used to be again.

Melissa had a bucket list party at our house for a large group of her psychologist colleagues. They were a well-educated group of really nice people and I liked all of them. They were laughing and talking as we went around the room reading the first item on our lists. The first guy wanted to airboat on the Amazon. A woman wanted to horseback ride on the beach on the Costa del Sol. Lists included tattoos, great dinners, exotic travel, same sex weddings, and jamming with John Legend.

As we went around the circle, I was near the end. I read the top item on my list: "To awaken to the reality of my spiritual life with

God." You could hear a chair creak as someone shifted their weight. Mine was the only wish out of fourteen that was met with dead silence. I saw I was already living in a different world from them. I had publicly outed myself. Then the game went on.

I went to see my doctor to renew my Adderall prescription. Adderall is a central nervous system (CNS) stimulant I was taking to balance out my attention deficit disorder. This time when he put the stethoscope on my chest, the doctor held it in one spot and his eyebrows went down in concentration. He said he noticed an arrhythmia, an irregular heartbeat. More specifically, he said it sounded like tachycardia, or an overly fast heartbeat. I had noticed this flutter in my chest occasionally throughout my life. My father said he had one and not to worry about it.

However, my doctor said, "Adults on CNS stimulant therapy have increased risk of having other cardiovascular risk factors." Hence, I needed to monitor my heartbeat over a period of time by wearing a Holter monitor.

I tried three times to make appointments to pick up the Holter monitor and failed each time. I didn't want to wear it anyhow and interpreted this difficulty in doing so as a sign that I didn't need it. The Course says that the laws of medicine are false. I decided to skip the Holter monitor and to cut back on all my medications. I did cut back and experienced no ill effects.

My dentist, however, after looking at the new wear patterns on my teeth, said that, from the wear patterns, he could tell that I was clenching and grinding my teeth during my sleep. He said stress and anxiety were the usual cause. To prevent wearing my teeth down he prescribed a plastic "night guard" which he custom fitted to my lower teeth. I then put it in my mouth every night. I must have been unconsciously stressed about something.

In March, I went to a two-week devotional retreat at the Living Miracles Center in Utah. On the last afternoon, David showed us the movie, *Brother Son, Sister Moon*, which was about Saint Francis and the founding of the Franciscan Order. Francis loved small creatures like birds and the people that society had forgotten. The brothers worked, laughed, and sang together. Afterward, David spoke more about his Living Miracles Center community. There were many parallels with the Franciscans, two communities devoted to service to God. In the evening all the retreat participants sang around the campfire in the canyon. I sat there after the singing was over and looked up at the sky, a very dark blue with billions of stars, some twinkling. I was sitting next to Willow, and we began talking.

"This way of life is so beautiful," she said. "It feels God-given. I've made up my mind. I'm going to leave my husband, the Shoshone tribe, my tribal lands, and come and join this community."

"I've also given it a lot of thought," I said. "David speaks with the voice of Jesus. It seems like Jesus has returned and we are so fortunate to be here for it. I'm going to leave my wife and family and come out here to join this community."

Now I was certain. This was the direction in which I unequivocally wanted to move my life. Joining Living Miracles would mean devoting my whole life to God and serving David and the Messengers.

When I got back to New Hampshire, Melissa was shocked and hoped it wasn't true, that I could still be turned back. She took me to see her therapist, Gary, a Buddhist and a psychotherapist for whom I had the highest respect. Yet I now saw him differently. Melissa and Gary told me I could have it all, the happiness and love I was seeking, without having to bring an abstract God into it. When they paused and invited me to speak, I confidently said that I truly loved Melissa *and* that God was primary for me. It turned out talking about God was a good way to bring earthly reasoned arguments to a close.

The next morning Melissa asked me why I wasn't sleeping with her. I told her I had stopped taking my medication for depression and my sleep pattern was affected. Melissa was upset and asked if there was anything else I had been afraid to tell her. So, I told her about the retreat and that I planned to return to the Living Miracles Center for several months this spring.

"Several months! Where did this come from? What about me, your wife? What about your son? He worships you. What about our life together?" She began to cry. "This is a hard way to be losing my husband, who doesn't even seem to care for me anymore."

Seeing her genuine upset, I felt compassion for her. I took her hand and we talked about our marriage, expectations, and plans. We went upstairs. I told her that I loved her, was happy with her and would never want to marry anyone else. But I also said that for the last twenty years, since God saved my life with AA and *A Course in Miracles,* I'd been getting closer and closer to Him. I knew God loved me, and I felt He was calling me. I began to cry about the loss of our marriage relationship, tearing up every time I thought about how great it had been, what an innocent person she was. But I also said God was my absolute choice. I added that God loved her maximally, regardless of what she thought or did. We held each other for a long time on the bed. She felt good to hold.

I still couldn't sleep that night and edited a video for David instead.

The next morning, I was aware of being angry at the noise my neighbor's truck was making. After a bit, I caught myself and realized I was doing it to myself, which didn't make me feel any better. But then I thought of really being God's Son, perfect, loved, innocent, and needing to do nothing, and I felt more at peace. I could see the shortcomings of my special relationship with Melissa. She definitely rained on my spiritual parade. Sex was no longer of interest to me. I wanted to keep my focus on Spirit.

Over the next week, in preparation for a move to Utah and to get rid of symbols of a past that didn't really exist, I threw out boxes of books and boxes of memorabilia, photographs, letters, degrees, files, most of which I used to consider treasures for my future admirers and biographers. The magnitude of my belief in the fake hit me. I took it all to the dump. As I heaved the bags into the huge bin, I had the thought, *This sure be better be the right decision, since I'm trashing my earthly life.* Then I thought that these must be the very things holding me down.

Melissa did a little cooking and washed some dishes. I realized I resented doing all of it while she was working. In any case I was looking forward to leaving this role-ridden house. I saw roles as ego constructions to hold us in place.

On Thursday afternoon Melissa again took me to see her psychotherapist. Gary questioned me almost rapid-fire. Yes, Melissa was a good wife. Yes, I found her to be attractive. Yes, she earned a lot of money as a combined ARNP and PhD psychotherapist. No, there wasn't another woman in Utah. Yes, I realized that she was okay with me not working for an extended period. And many similar questions. It was clear that Gary couldn't believe that I was planning to leave Melissa.

"So, what on earth makes you want to leave her, to leave your whole life behind?"

I told them that God was calling me out of the world and that I had unequivocally answered, "Yes!" This represented the end of our marriage, as we had known it. *I've done it, I've cast my lot with God and David.*

Later, at home, Melissa asked, "What do you really want?"

"The peace of God," I replied without hesitation.

"Well then you're on your own." Melissa, fighting back tears, left the house and went for a long drive.

I was glad to have everything perfectly clear between us. I felt lighter.

From my journal April 14, 2011:

I took no antidepressant pills this morning. Have felt dizzy and pretty much been sleeping or lying down all the time since. Last night, in a long dream, I brought about peace between Hitler and his people in a personal, low-key way; by the end of the dream, I was babysitting his daughter. This morning I wasn't able to read computer screens (quite dizzy with significant distortions of my visual field), so I listened to my Course-related songs, laughing and crying easily, which was fun. I'm still sleeping a lot, dizzy, and having the experience of a kind of skipping in my head, as if the electricity is knocked out for half a second, accompanied by a slight static puff in my ears. I'm spacey and absent-minded.

The next morning, I was guided first to some spiritual music and then to the online Spiritual Mind Training Program, where I was working through the Forgiveness section. Melissa had been crying, and she came over to talk to me. She made various statements and asked me some questions. Throughout, I kept forgiveness in the front of my mind. "Forgiveness is still and quietly does nothing, welcoming truth exactly as it is." (ACIM) I also thought to give each holy instant over to the Holy Spirit and followed Him in my gentle responses to Melissa. And I remembered that "I am God's Son, complete and healed and whole, shining in the reflection of His Love," and therefore, so is Melissa. We are innocent and healed. She became calm, stopped crying, and went to take a shower.

Compiling David's book, I read in the chapter on Love, "Love is not personal or specific. It is impossible to love something specific, for Love is Whole and knows no parts. God being Love, is One and abstract." and "The world is nothing but a representation of private thoughts."

In the chapter "Perceive the Body or Behold the Spirit," David says, "It helps to keep in mind that people aren't really people, they are thoughts" and further "Relationship is not personal. Holy relationship is not between people." All of this spoke against my empathic values and earthly relationship with Melissa.

The Course says, "The special relationships of the world are destructive, selfish, and childishly egocentric. Yet, if given to the Holy Spirit, these relationships can become the holiest things on earth, the miracles that point the way to the return to heaven. The special love relationship is the ego's most boasted gift, and one which has the most appeal to those unwilling to relinquish guilt. The 'dynamics' of the ego are clearest here, for counting on the attraction of this offering, the fantasies that center around it are often quite overt." So much for romantic love. So much for my special love relationship with Melissa. Following the Course, I steeled myself against feeling love for her.

The Course goes on to say, "You really think you are alone unless another body is with you. Think further; you believe in the 'laws' of friendship, of good relationships and reciprocity." The Course says that none of these are true. Hence, devoted students of the Course do not seek out friends. They let existing friendships slide. When not working, they spend much of their time alone.

David and the Messengers were telling me that I was in a special relationship which was of the ego. They counseled me over the phone that I was to leave home, leave all my possessions, sever my relationships with my friends and family, and drive to Utah to join the community. My wife took me to see her therapist one last time. I told them both that I felt called by God, that this was the truth and that I was going to do it no matter what.

On May 16, 2011, I took Melissa and Evan out to dinner at a favorite Mexican restaurant in Manchester. I told them I was leaving the next morning, that I had been called by God to join the Living Miracles community in Utah.

"That's not fair!" said Melissa. "I love you; you have a loving family here; we don't want you to go. You can't just leave us!"

"I love you too, and my leaving for Utah doesn't end that. I have been called to something higher."

"This just isn't rational. Why don't you just visit there for another three weeks or a month if you feel you have to. What about us?" Melissa said, and she started to cry loud enough that people at other tables turned to look at us. This was not going the way I had hoped.

"God will take care of all of us. You'll see that this is all for the best."

"Da-ad," Evan said, in a tone that said, *Come on, be reasonable.*

But I was intransigent. Melissa continued to plead, her eyes red with crying. I imagined that she was a temptress of the ego, trying to keep the Son of God from his true calling.

I didn't want this scene to get out of hand. I was embarrassed and angry yet determined. I decided to cut the meal short and got the check.

The next day, I loaded some clothes and belongings into my car, left my wife crying in the driveway, and set out for Utah. I drove most of the way through Pennsylvania and checked into a motel as it began to get dark. In my room, I opened my suitcase, I saw that Melissa had stuck two framed family pictures on top. Thinking she (the ego) was trying to divert me from my mission, I threw them in the trash.

I spoke with David on the phone once a day during the trip, and he encouraged me along the way. I also had a long playlist of Course-related music and some of David's talks to listen to as I drove. I was excited about this life change. Along the way, I stopped and visited with two of David's friends and talked with them about my spiritual adventure. I was revved.

10.

Initial Success at Living Miracles

I arrived at the Living Miracles Center in Utah as planned on May 20, 2011. I was full of happy energy. I felt I was in the Promised Land. The Strawberry Canyon even looked like the Holy Land. It was high elevation desert with aromatic sagebrush and stunted pinion pine trees scattered at random. The ice-cold Strawberry River flowed swiftly through the canyon over a rocky bed, making a dramatic temperature contrast with the hot, dry desert air. The river came from under a huge dam about five miles upstream.

At the Living Miracles Center, the valley widened and was bordered on both sides by steep sandstone walls. The Center itself consisted of several rustic buildings on the rim of the south cliff. The views were spectacular. It was like being in a mini–Grand Canyon. One afternoon when I was down in the canyon, I heard the drums of the Unitah Indian tribe coming down from their reservation on the other side of the north wall of the canyon. I was reminded of Carlos Castaneda's book, *The Teachings of Don Juan: a Yaqui Way of Knowledge,* in which a Yaqui Indian introduces a white student to spiritual experiences through eating peyote, the hallucinogenic mushrooms.

I had been preparing for this big shift in my life since I met David Hoffmeister in 2004. Since then, I had been actively reading everything he wrote, listening to his audios and watching every one of his videos. I even wrote a collection of summaries of all of his videos that was used by the Messengers in developing the flagship Spiritual Mind Training program. This two-year online training program was used by David's students all over the world. I was considered a "community member" of Living Miracles.

At the Living Miracles Center, I lived in the men's bunk. My primary jobs, which I did as a volunteer, included recording David's speaking engagements with a movie camera, both at the Living Miracles Center and when he travelled, then editing and enhancing the videos and uploading them to David's free YouTube channel and to his paid subscription channel. I also edited audio files of David's talks for Spreaker, an online audio library, adjusting the sound levels for the best auditory experience. I edited written transcripts of David's talks, of which there were a great many, and turned them into published materials that were posted online and included in his books. I took pride in being able to do these things well, as though I owned a bit of the spiritual content. Still, my work was not acknowledged. And I wanted acknowledgment.

So, I was learning new skills, had a renewed sense of purpose, and was excited at being able to reach a huge audience. On David's websites, we practiced search engine optimization. This is the process of maximizing the number of visitors to a website. In my personal life, however, I dramatically reduced the frequency of my communications with Melissa and Evan.

David Hoffmeister was a good speaker. He never used any notes. The message seemed to come from the Holy Spirit through David. He used personal examples, made eye contact, and told stories that were genuinely funny and laughed. When transcribing his talks, however, I had to pay attention to the significant difference between the spoken word and written text. Written texts do not include smiles and frowns. Some common utterances such as "and ah" need to be deleted, as do sentences that are half-started and then revised.

It was part of my job to edit such things out of the videos. This was a challenge because the audio track is linked to the video, so to simply cut some audio out of the track would make a jump in the visual action. At such times it was good to have two cameras going. I could make the cut at the same time I switched from camera 1 to camera 2. I also perfected using a close-up camera and a profile camera, switching back and forth between them in order to help the viewer maintain interest in what was being said. I was always interested in what he said.

I learned to put subscription links into videos, use title screens and titles in different ways, add theme songs, and offer a half-dozen cross-links at the end. These allowed viewers to see how broad Living Miracles' offerings were in videos, participatory programs, books and pamphlets, audios, and even an extensive guide to movie watching with spiritual interpretations.

Toward the beginning of my stay at Living Miracles Center in Utah, a volunteer named Mateo arrived from Guatemala. He was a good deal younger than me, very handsome with thick black hair and sunglasses that made him look like a movie star. Although he was intelligent and fluent in English, he was humble and eager to learn. We began taking long walks in the evening together, talking about life, spirituality, family, and women.

At one point he said he was still married to a woman living in

New Hampshire. So was I! In my enthusiasm, I interpreted this coincidence as a positive sign about our friendship. Mateo had met Candace online and had visited her in New Hampshire several times. But the relationship was over; they both wanted out but hadn't gotten around to the paperwork. Mateo and I loved taking long walks together through the bottom of the canyon, following the river, sometimes for miles into the night. One night, under a sky resplendent with myriad huge stars, he told me about a dream he had just had in which he was a biblical figure interacting with John the Baptist. Mateo was powerfully moved by it. I was happy for him and encouraged him to share it with David. He did so the next day, but David did not give it much weight.

Several months later, however, Maria Hernandez, who had now become a Messenger, told me and Mateo that we should stop all this walking and talking. I believe this was because she thought we were forming a "special relationship," which we were. I knew special relationships were in a sense forbidden, but my friendship with Mateo seemed so innocent and so helpful to our growing spirituality that we couldn't stop talking to each other. We just tried to keep it out of sight.

David purchased a house in Salt Lake City and a large former inn in Kamas to hold the growing community and have better internet connection. I made substantial financial contributions to these projects.

I was called upon to lead discussion groups on *A Course in Miracles* and David's teachings. I led groups in person for local people and on Zoom for far-flung audiences. They were well attended, usually around twelve people. Participants found their understanding of the spirituality described in ACIM and David's work was clarified and sometimes taken to a deeper level. This gave me a sense of satisfaction.

For a while I also accepted telephone counseling calls from people experiencing some form of distress. I would listen closely, ask a few follow-up questions, join with them in prayer. Then I would clearly restate their basic question aloud to the Holy Spirit. Then we would pray in silence, waiting for some spiritual insight to the problem. After a couple minutes, I would ask them what they got by way of an answer. Often something would have come to them, and I would reinforce their intuition about what they had received. Then I would offer what I understood to be the Holy Spirit's message, usually something related to trust and healing.

For a month or two I even had the distinction of offering the Sunday service at the Living Miracles Center. People from the Kamas area would join in attending along with our community members. I would pick a theme from the Course, develop it a bit and then give an example of its application, theoretical or practical as the case might be. Often, I would play a spiritual song that related. There were a great many spiritual/new age songs by artists such as Kirtana to choose from.

On one of these occasions, when I was feeling particularly inspired, I gave a talk that started with something from Jesus in the Course, went full circle and came back to a resounding call to Jesus. I felt powerful and was a little surprised at myself. This talk was noted by the Messenger present, Janet, who then gave a glowing report of it to David. Not long after that I was made a licensed minister, which is just below an ordained minister. An or-dained minister can marry people. But that Sunday service was about as high as I flew.

I must say that the Messengers and those around David were, in general, a highly intelligent bunch. Their thinking aligned with the Course, which had come as a sort of automatic dictation to Helen Schucman, a brilliant psychologist in New York City. The Course she scribed is a challenging read. It also has daily lessons, which everyone at Living Miracles did on their own.

David surrounded himself with people who were very tech savvy to run his vast Internet ministry. He had more than ten websites, each with a different emphasis. We did a lot of work developing, expanding, and linking these websites.

I didn't like to think about it, but I was jealous of Messengers like Jeff who communicated frequently and easily with David. Jeff was a guitar player/singer who had formerly been a hypnotherapist. He had an easy rapport with David, and it seemed whenever Jeff had a question about something significant, he'd call David. I guess I had low spiritual esteem. I thought my concerns didn't really matter and that I should work them out with the inner voice of the Holy Spirit and a Messenger, rather than bothering David. I was also afraid to make a mistake. I didn't want to reveal my ignorance in an area I was unsure about because I was afraid of being spiritually wrong.

There was one time when I challenged David. He and some Messengers had gone off and purchased about eight huge luxury recliners for the main room, which we called the sanctuary. It was a very large, beautiful room with huge windows looking out on the courtyard. The volunteers were only allowed into the sanctuary at certain times. There was a general meeting and I spoke up about what I saw as an apparent gross inequality, fostered by David, between the Messengers and the volunteers. The Messengers had large private bedrooms, most with private bathrooms. The volunteers were crammed into the men's or women's bunk.

I spoke up loudly, with a strain in my voice that I wished wasn't there. "This is unfair—these huge luxurious chairs for Messengers. Where is the equality of the sons of God? We shouldn't be encouraging separation and hierarchies."

There was a silence, and I knew several of the volunteers were thinking along the same lines I was. But David just picked up where he had left off talking about some spiritual topic. I soon noticed that I was feeling very uncomfortable and that feeling progressed to feeling overcome by the thought that David was right and that I had been wrong.

I spoke up again and said, "I'm sorry, I was wrong. David knows what is best for all of us." And my voice deteriorated, and I could no longer speak because I was crying.

About once a week, David would show a movie to the Messengers and volunteers living in the Kamas Living Miracles Center. We would be in the sanctuary, a large room in this French Provincial-style house with a high ceiling and four tall windows that looked out on the courtyard. I often pulled the large burgundy curtains to darken the room. One of our tech wizards would project the movie. We would bring in popcorn or a snack and sit on cushions on the floor, or if not occupied by a Messenger, the recliner chairs. There might be fifteen of us. Following the movie, David would give us the Holy Spirit's interpretation of the movie. This was often very insightful. Then we would offer our thoughts and impressions of the film and how it spoke to spirit's presence.

Unhappily after a while, I again experienced having my thoughts ignored—the silence with which my comments were met at movie gatherings indicated that my thoughts were deemed to be of the ego and not of the Holy Spirit. I stayed on, believing that with time I would begin to hear the voice of the Holy Spirit in my head. That never happened. My work was not appreciated even though it was good work. It seemed my ego was not to be fed in any way.

My lived experience at Living Miracles was dissonant with my conception of a loving spiritual community. Although David spoke against the "special relationship," his bed was consistently occupied by one female Messenger after another. I was no longer excited about my video-editing work. Rather, I just did it as a repetitious chore. It seemed I'd already heard David's messages. Although I partnered with another volunteer each morning to go over the daily ACIM lesson, I was no longer anticipating a spiritual awakening. After a few years of living in Utah I gradually began to become depressed.

David never once mentioned my book, *Creating Harmonious Relationships*. In fact, no one had any interest in what I had done previously. Empathic methods of communication were seen simply as egoic demonstrations and hence valueless. The only valuable word was that of the Holy Spirit. The Messengers claimed to hear the voice of the Holy Spirit and David claimed to hear the voice of Jesus himself. I had noticed several occasions when it was obvious that what the Messengers were saying was not the Word of God. This would become apparent in specific situations, such as car repair. But it would not be acceptable to challenge them. I wanted to stay. I held on to the idea that if I reversed *my* thinking, truly gave my life over to God, that I would be enveloped in God's love. It might happen tomorrow.

But I clearly was not hearing a voice in my head. I thought/ hoped that my intuitive hunches were effectively guided by the Holy Spirit, but the Messengers would give direction. They were hearing the Holy Spirit and I wasn't. My depression deepened.

I was frequently encouraged to dismantle my ego. I thought of what I still had in a physical sense that supported my egoic pride. I had the seven remaining copies of my book plus two binders. The first binder held reviews and praise for my book from all over the world. The second held letters of appreciation that I had received from clients during the various phases of my professional life. Yes, flipping through them I did get a feeling of pride. But now I was in the new world of Living Miracles. I had to remember that here I knew nothing and that my contributions were meaningless. I took the books and binders and one by one threw them into a blazing in- cinerator. I felt sad watching my worldly achievements burn, curling up page by page, in the hot red light of the fire.

Why had I submitted? Why did I drop my goal of being loved, loving others, and helping others to communicate in a loving way? Because I wanted David's approval. I strived for years to get it from David, and I never got it. I sold my soul to David seeking it. His "no people-pleasing" guideline was the antithesis of my core value: forming loving connections through empathic communication.

One evening David showed the movie *Meru*, which chronicles three mountain climbers' attempts to scale this most dangerous

Himalayan summit. They struggled to overcome an avalanche, critical injury, and their own past climbing traumas. The victory I saw for these fanatical climbers was making it out alive.

After viewing the movie, the Living Miracles community members present talked about being strong representatives of the Son of God and not kowtowing to human foibles and weaknesses.

Two days later, Kyle, a tall, lean Messenger with big ears that stood out from his head, offered to lead a hike along a relatively untraveled stream in northwestern Utah. Seven of us accepted the offer, some long-term volunteers like me and some more short-term visitors to the community. Rhonda was an older woman who had been sharing with the community for a long time via the internet.

It was a long ride in the van to get there, but it was a fine day with a few puffy white clouds in a clear blue sky. There were cottonwood trees along the banks. Kyle led us downstream on a rough, fairly steep trail for about two hours. It became hot. Finally, we stopped for a little lunch by a lovely pool in the stream. Then Kyle set off on the return trip. He set a brisk pace. Rhonda and another woman began to fall behind. I mentioned this to Kyle, and he replied, with a determined expression looking upstream, "This is a good pace." He reminded me of a British officer in India, out of touch with and not particularly caring about the people in the situation at hand.

I became concerned for the two women, that they might fall very far behind and get hurt or lost. So I slowed down to keep them in sight. After a while they stopped to rest. I went back and sat with them. I pointed out that we were far behind, but they said they were doing their best.

I stuck with them as we set off again upstream. Kyle must have been way ahead by then. After a while, heavy clouds rolled in, and it began to get dark early. Rhonda was going slowly, complaining about a bad knee. As the daylight trickled away, I became concerned we'd get trapped by nightfall. I became more aware of how rocky the trail was. Occasionally a rock would begin to roll when I stepped on it. It would be so easy to sprain an ankle. Should there be an accident, the logistics of trying to carry someone out were daunting.

Finally, I heard talking up ahead and then the parking area came into view. Kyle hardly acknowledged us. I thought Kyle would lead the group in a processing discussion about the hike. I had a grievance about Kyle's hard-driving leadership and was hoping for some explanation. But Kyle just called out, "Okay, everyone, let's head back to the Center." The very tired ladies thanked me, and we got in the van and left.

As we rode back, the thought that kept coming to my mind about Kyle was "that asshole." He was probably thirty years younger than those women, but he made no accommodation for their age. I couldn't figure it out. Was his keeping a fast pace a lesson for us, that we all needed to abandon our limitations and keep up? Forget it. I think *Meru* had gone to his head.

Along the same line of *shape up or ship out*, I remember sitting at lunch in the Center and mentioning the depression I was dealing with. Olivia barked out, "Andy, this isn't a hospital." End of discussion.

We were all encouraged to say what we felt we needed to say regardless of other peoples' feelings. A few months later I was sitting at a small dinner table with Janet and a few of the volunteers. A leathery volunteer with a stubbly face looked at me and said, "Damn it. I'm sick of your whining. Why don't you go and join that dead brother of yours?" I was shocked and hurt. I looked at Janet to say something, but she wouldn't make eye contact, tacitly agreeing with him. Well, damn them. I got up and went to the bunkroom. I was shaking with anger at them and sorry for myself that I was stuck in such an unfeeling place.

I thought of leaving. But I felt I had made a lifelong, 100 percent commitment. And of course, to cement that I left my wife and family. Over the years of studying the Course I had let all my friends go. I had signed aboard this ship as an able-bodied seaman and it was on the high sea, headed I knew not where.

Each morning the steward, the Messenger in charge of a Living Miracles center, assigned tasks to the volunteers. After a huge two-foot snowfall in Utah, Olivia asked me to shovel out the parking area, by myself. The snow blower had been done-in by a previous volunteer. The gravel parking area was large, and there was no place to put the snow without carrying each shovelful fifty feet or so. It was a huge job and there were four shovels. I asked Olivia to take a look at the scope of the job and she refused. She just said, "You shovel it." So, I spent over half the day carrying shovels full of snow and throwing them over the bank until it was done. I was fatigued and, in spite of it being very cold out, drenched in sweat. Yet at the end, there was no acknowledgment or thanks.

David spoke out against having health insurance. *A Course in Miracles* states that the rules of medicine did not apply to us as spirit. So, I got rid of my health insurance. Later I learned David carried his own health insurance policy and used it with reasonable frequency.

A Course in Miracles states that its goal is "mind training," learning to listen to the voice of the Holy Spirit and not the voice of the ego. David had a group of twelve Messengers who could hear the voice of the Holy Spirit. They told the rest of us who were not hearing the Voice of the Holy Spirit what to do. The aim of the "mind training" for us was to "dismantle the ego." In essence this came down to not trusting our own minds, our opinions and intuitions. The message was repeated to me that I had nothing to contribute and should just take orders from the Messengers.

To help dismantle my ego and increase my humility, in the summer I was asked to perform regular tasks such as lawn mowing, weed whacking, pool and hot tub cleaning and maintenance, sweeping, vacuuming, and dishwashing. After a while, my depression really kicked in. I got so down I couldn't cook a full meal for myself, so I copied what others cooked. I could manage cereal and a banana for breakfast.

David had a different view of money and morality. All the money taken in from volunteers' rental payments and retreat payments went to David and the dissemination of his teachings. I paid $1000 a month for room and board. Sometimes David bought a house or larger estate, to which I'd make a hefty contribution as I wanted to use it up for spiritual purposes.

One day I asked David what he would do if he were in the bank and a teller accidentally gave him an extra hundred-dollar bill: Would he keep it or point out the teller's mistake and give it back?

He replied, "I would keep it, that is God's money." God's money and David's money evidently being one and the same.

In the midst of my depression, Olivia called upon me to travel to the island of Grand Canaria, Spain, to find a place for a European center of the community. David had previously held what he called a highly successful retreat there. So, depressed as I was, I got on a plane and flew there. But it turned out there was no welcome for me or Living Miracles. I traveled around with two women volunteers as we looked for possible locations in Gran Canaria. Finding none, I responded to a call from a friend on the mainland in Spain. She thought there might be a suitable location near her in her town, which was near Malaga.

So, the three of us flew to Malaga. I picked up the airfare. That building didn't work out. We searched around for a couple weeks and finally found the perfect place, a large villa on a hillside with a swimming pool in front and orange groves in back. I was glad the search was over as I was becoming glum and downhearted. Finally, Olivia allowed me to fly back to Utah. There was no appreciation for me on finding a beautiful villa for Living Miracles to use as a European base.

For quite a while life was uneventful at the Kamas Living Miracles Center. The rules were strict for the volunteers or "lifers" as we were nicknamed. One rule we all followed was to not engage in any contact with our former family and friends. The volunteers had a separate wing of the building with bunkbeds and were not allowed into more comfortable parts of the building except to clean. Even the kitchen was closed off except for us to make our meals at mealtime.

We even needed permission from the Messenger in charge to

take a walk. I would take long walks by myself often in the late afternoon when my video editing was done for the day. I liked to walk along the river. The ground was gravelly a with tufts of dry, yellow grass scattered around and very occasionally a clump of cottonwood trees. I walked in silence or listened to Course-related audios. I was always seeking to allow the Course view of life and relationships to permeate me. Always checking my mind for insights or intuitions that could be attributed to the Holy Spirit. Yet always feeling insecure, that the Holy Spirit didn't deem me worthy to communicate with.

I had stopped taking my antidepressants, and it caught up with me. I was following Course lesson 76 which says,

> You really think a small round pellet, or some fluid pushed into your veins through a sharpened needle will ward off disease and death. It is insanity that thinks these things. You call them laws and put them under different names in a long catalogue of rituals that have no use and serve no purpose. You think you must obey the laws of medicine, of economics and of health. Protect the body, and you will be saved. These are not laws, but madness.

Without the medication, I fell into deep depression. I felt like jumping off the rim of the canyon and splattering on the rocks below or even driving my car off the cliff. It was quite possible, but remembering that automatic air bags would deploy, I gave up on that idea. I began to feel paranoid, that the others could read my mind and would prevent me from running and jumping. I thought about it a lot.

I was going through a dark night of the soul and wanting a major boost in my spiritual life when Maria Hernandez invited me to join her in Spain. She had gone there to head the new Living Miracles Center after Chloé had taken over her place in David's bed. In Spain, Maria took up with a handsome volunteer from Sweden. This was the villa with swimming pool and orange orchard that I had previously found.

I arrived in Malaga still fearful and doubting my worthiness, but with a strong desire to heal my mind. I found that my companions, my projects and tasks, and the experiential sessions offered by the stewards all helped me to share, build trust and heal my mind.

One night Maria showed the Walt Disney movie *Tangled,* which is about a girl, kidnapped at birth, who one day discovers that she is really a beloved princess. Maria shared the experience she had had identifying with the movie and the Course. And I felt it too! I had the profound experience that "I am the holy Son of God Himself," that that was who I really was, my glorious identity being fixed and unchangeable. Whew! I relaxed. I saw I could take my little ego self more lightly, no longer needing to judge it or to strive to improve it. It was much more fun to hold the Son of God perspective and be joyful.

I began to really enjoy gardening, swimming and hanging out at the pool, dancing freely, squeezing fresh orange juice, and cooking with others. I felt grateful to the community and to Maria for the empathy extended to me. Under Maria's kind rule, and restarting antidepressants, I gradually got better.

After three months, our Spanish visas expired. Maria and I then flew to Prague to help out a Course student, Scott, who wanted to have English-language movie sessions at his apartment in downtown Prague. We led a small but intimate movie gathering that helped boost Scott's spirits and paved the way for future endeavors.

Then Maria and I flew to England where we led some course gatherings in Cornwall and southern England. I particularly liked these gatherings as the people were native speakers and I could make a lot of jokes, which I did very successfully. Maria was impressed with my ability to sense where the crowd was at and to tell amusing Course-related stories. She helped me remember to drive our rental car on the left side of the road, especially at roundabouts.

At this time, I received an invitation from Chloé to fly to Hawaii, where she was in charge of a new Living Miracles Center. She had recently left David's bedroom and was now in a relationship with Kyle. Chloé had very short hair and a strong gymnast's body. She was from France and spoke with a pronounced French accent.

I arrived on the Big Island of Hawaii and went to our center in Pahoa. The landscape was lush rainforest, but it only rained during the night. Coqui frogs began croaking early in the evening and lasted long into the night. They were like a lullaby but made evening recording sessions of David all but impossible. There were avocado and mango trees on the property, as well as tangy-delicious *lilikoi*, or passionfruit. I learned to split coconuts with a single stroke of my machete and could swing on jungle vines *à la* Tarzan. I was frequently engaged in building fences to keep out the wild pigs with their menacing-looking tusks. They only attempted encroachment on our lawns and gardens at night. I visited the Kilauea volcano and saw its shimmering, red-hot molten lava.

David and the Messengers had a large house on the ocean they called the temple. A couple of us would go over there once a week to clean it. The timid little green-gray geckos that, from time to time, crawled around the walls and ceiling amused me. They live together with people without harm and do a great job eating cockroaches, ants, and spiders. The geckos seem to defy gravity because they have expanded toe pads with microscopic hairlike structures that cling to any surface. I looked it up.

Hawaii was a benevolent place to serve the Messengers. I edited David's videos all day and took long walks in the late afternoon. I was selected to lead a weekly ACIM discussion group for people on the Big Island. An Australian volunteer, Caleb, had some profound forgiveness experiences, during which he cried and wailed on the carpet. Afterward, he said he had really had a breakthrough and that his life was no longer the same. This inspired me. I felt I needed to get more in touch with my emotions.

I again chose to go off my antidepression medications so that I might get in touch with my feelings and get the transcendent spiritual experience of God's love, which I so desperately sought. But it remained elusive.

After about a year, the decision was made to sell the Hawaii center and I received an invitation to join a new center in Chapala, Mexico. The center was stewarded by Emma Davis, who was a delightful leader whom I had admired for a long time. Emma was not a Messenger because, in spite of her grasp of ACIM metaphysics and practice, she still had a lot of money and a large property in Australia. It was the practice that Messengers gave over everything they owned to David when he appointed them a Messenger.

Chapala is a quaint town on the shore of Lake Chapala. As a

result of its high altitude, the climate is perfect. There is a brief rainy season with dramatic thunderstorms which, maybe once a year, turn the road into a river. I floated down it one time in flood season, past the center, in an inner tube. The local food was delicious and inexpensive, both in the markets and the restaurants. One day I was caught by a heavy rainstorm about a quarter of a mile from our center. I ducked into a little shop and the owner gave me her umbrella to get home, because she recognized that we were "vecinos," neighbors. I felt truly welcome there.

The Center itself was as large as a city block, surrounded by an eight-foot brick wall and twenty-five-foot palm trees. Inside was a beautifully landscaped garden paradise. There were lush lawns bordered by exotic flowers blooming at different times of year: Mexican sunflowers, orchids, honeysuckles, marigolds, poinsettias, a zillion little flowers and cacti. There were red banana palm trees that produced more fruit in season than we could possibly eat, so we gave it away. There was a full-size swimming pool with a terrace. Next to it was a thatched *palapa*, open on the sides, and comfortable pool chairs The low brick buildings holding the kitchen and bunkrooms with terracotta roofs had windows and even several glass sliders. David had a huge bedroom on the second floor of the Messengers' building with windows looking out over the lake. We had gardens in back, one of which we turned over to growing squash and beans.

This was probably my happiest time in the community. Emma and I made some very creative videos; one in particular featured rotating pictures of David and community members to the tune of "*Feliz Navidad*." We enjoyed swimming in the pool, walking along the *malecón* of Lake Chapala, eating dinner in town, and running errands around the area in the Messenger car.

A genuine friendship flourished between me and Emma. She was a straight person, which is to say not spiritual in such a way as to create a separation from others. We would collaborate in my room on any writing either of us had to do. One day Emma, who had recently returned from a visit to her home in Australia, said she missed being held. So, I invited her to lie on the bed with me and I held her. It felt very relaxing for both of us. We had been strictly cautioned by Messenger Sophia, however, not to have a sexual relationship. Nonetheless a little yes/no went on in my head as I felt Emma breathing against my chest. Sadly, it ended in no. I had left my wife for Living Miracles, and I was not about to imperil the whole thing by starting another special relationship. Above all I wanted to follow the letter of David's instructions for awakening.

Emma and I went to the outdoor markets on Wednesday in old town Chapala. The food there was fresher and much less expensive than in the supermarket. A long cobblestone street was lined with food stalls piled high with fresh vegetables. The vendors would call out their prices. Sometimes there was a mariachi band, and always a bustling crowd of customers. Many of the food vendors we saw every week would chat it up and offer us specials. It seemed they were always smiling and laughing. Sometimes avocados were not in season or maybe one of the trucks didn't make it. In that case, we would go up and down the length of the street to find who was selling good-quality avocados at the best price.

In Mexico, foreign nationals who do not have a permanent resident visa, must leave every six months and refresh their visas when they return across the border. Rather than going to the United States, I chose to fly to Guatemala City and have a reunion for three days with Mateo. It was great to see him—we had a big, long hug. He took me out to lunch where he introduced me to his new girlfriend, Regina. Mateo was an excellent artist with ballpoint pen. Regina had been one of his models. The three of us went to the trendy neighborhood of Cayalá and took some hilarious selfies around the statue of a giant emerging from the earth. Then we sat in a courtyard and Mateo asked me if I would do some couples counseling with them. Mateo had read my book, *Creating Harmonious Relationships*. I did listen and counsel, and evidently my counseling was effective because Mateo and Regina are still happily together.

11.

Going Deeper

At the time I began this venture in 2011, before leaving home for the Living Miracles Center in Utah, my young adult son, Evan, was having serious problems with alcohol and heroin. I found myself in the rescuer role, even picking him up at the police station when he was caught driving while intoxicated. I earnestly tried to help him. I talked with him about my experience with alcohol and drugs. I got him lists of AA meetings, Narcotics Anonymous meetings, and rehabilitation programs. I even brought him with me to some AA meetings, being careful not to embarrass him concerning our father and son relationship. I offered to pay for methadone or other rehab programs and that was frustrating for me. But I also realized that he needed to find his own program and his own sponsor.

One morning when I was still in New Hampshire I was driving Evan to work because his license had been suspended. As we neared his workplace he said, "You don't have to bother picking me up because Ralph is going to pick me up with my car after work."

"Who's Ralph?"

"Ralph lives in my apartment." Pause. "But there's a problem." He wasn't looking at me.

"Yeah, what's that?" I rolled up my window to hear better.

"He's been stealing from me. I guess he comes into my room and steals money and shit."

"That's outrageous! What kind of creep is he?" I turned toward him.

"Well, there's a warrant out for his arrest."

"What? You shouldn't be living with this guy. You should throw him out of the place!"

"Yeah, well, I don't think it's that easy."

I wanted to protect my son. It seemed to me that Ralph might even be the source of Evan's drugs. I got the idea to set up a sting operation to bring Ralph to justice.

I drove into Manchester and found a uniformed police officer directing traffic not far from Evan's workplace. I stopped and talked to the officer, telling him I was going to deliver a wanted man, Ralph Jones, to him a little after five o'clock. Then I called Evan at work and told him that when Ralph came to pick him up, he should say *he* was going to drive and put Ralph in the passenger seat. Then as he drove down Mill Street, he should look for me waving my arms and pull over.

I then waited on Mill Street for Evan to appear. When his car came into sight, I waved him over to the side of the road and Evan pulled up between me and the police officer. I told the police officer that this was Ralph Jones, who was wanted on an arrest warrant. The officer had been joined by two more policemen to make the catch. One officer had Ralph turn around and put handcuffs on him. Yes! The first officer was doing a lot of talking on a two-way radio while the other checked all of our identifying information.

Then to my surprise, they put cuffs on Evan as well. This upset me, and I used every bit of self-control to appear calm and avoid messing up the operation. The officer explained that Evan's driver's license had been suspended for a DWI. So, he was driving against the law. My heart sank, I hadn't considered that. I explained to the officer that I had been the one to tell my son to drive in order to bring Ralph in. It seemed to take a long time as the officer talked on his radio.

Finally, they took the cuffs off Evan, gave him a stern warning, and let him go. They put Ralph, who had remained calm throughout, into the back seat of a police car and drove off with him. I drove Evan home to his apartment.

The next week I was giving him a ride when Evan casually mentioned that he was living with Ralph again. What! Wasn't he in jail? Evan said Ralph had spent two nights in jail and then they let him go. I guess they couldn't pin drug dealing on him. This was typical of my son during that part of his life, to take drugs and to run with a bad crowd.

Evan was upset when I packed up and moved to Utah. For three years there was almost no communication between us. He emailed that during that time his mother had taken him in and made him detox cold turkey in her house in rural New Hampshire.

I did feel guilty about leaving and was sad about the loss of connection. I missed him. But my commitment to spiritual awakening held steady. In my mind I saw Evan's essential innocence and wished him happiness. Hearing no other guidance, I left the relationship to the Holy Spirit.

Then I got this email from Evan.

Dad,

There are many things I've been wanting to say to you, but I'll just keep it brief for now.

I've come to realize that I've not been authentic with you or myself about your absence. I've been pretending that I don't miss you or that I don't care that we haven't been in touch for so long. I've also been blaming you for my own unhappiness.

The result of this has been a loss of love and connection between us.

I'm committed now to the possibility for us to be in open, honest, and loving communication, and to be in a place where I'm not blaming you or making you wrong, and instead being okay with you; both the way you are, and the way you're not. In this new space that we create, you will be free to do whatever you want to do with your life, and I will be okay with whatever that is.

Love,
Your Son

Wow! What a blessing! What a huge shift in my son, from resentment to acceptance! What a miracle!

I went to report this good news to Alice, the Messenger who was in charge at the time. Alice read the email with a slight smile.

"Isn't that great?" I ventured. "My son still loves me!"

"Yes, that's a good reflection of your mental state."

"*My* mental state, don't you mean *his* mental state."

"The Course text says that a change of attitude between two people can occur as easily when the interaction takes place in the mind as when it involves physical interaction."

"Oh yeah, a reflection of my mental state." I remembered. "But it's been three years. I was thinking I might fly back East for a quick visit."

"Andy, you know that special family relationships are of the ego, and it's really best to avoid them."

"But I feel like I want to do something to connect better with him. Just zip out on a plane for a quick visit."

"Actually, you don't need to *do* anything. The Course says so in several places. Let me look it up."

She flipped through the Course book. I knew what was coming.

"Here, it's even a chapter heading, 'I Need Do Nothing.' It continues, 'When peace comes at last... it always comes with just one happy realization: *I need do nothing.*'"

Alice looked up at me. I felt disappointed, knew she and the Course were right.

"Okay, I guess I can keep thinking and communicating lovingly with him."

"Exactly."

I wrote this email back to Evan:

Hi Evan,

   I am so happy to hear this! I welcome your invitation to be in open, honest, and loving communication. I have felt sad about our lack of communication and have thought that you resented me for going off to follow this path to awakening. (I feel a little embarrassed that I haven't awakened yet.)

I heard the Call three years ago and was guided to join the Living Miracles community to speed my waking from the dream.

I was depressed for a year, and for a year have been feeling better and better, so that now I can honestly say I feel great. Life is good in this community in Mexico, and I am able to focus on my purpose, which is healing my mind of false concepts and beliefs.

I want you to know that nothing will ever change the fact that I love you.

Love,

Dad

I thought the Holy Spirit must be behind Evan's psychological healing. So, I must heal this relationship from afar. I squashed my impulse to go and see him and tried to improve my relationship with him in my mind.

Yes, I *was* embarrassed that I had no sign of awakening, no profound mystical experience. I was enjoying life in Chapala, but I felt guilty. Had I made a huge mistake giving up everything, including the people in my life? I had talked on the phone a while back with Melissa about a divorce, and she said she had cried every day for a year after I left. I felt sad hearing this. We both cried on the phone. Yes, but she was part of the illusion.

The divorce was easily accomplished by mail as we were residents of New Hampshire. I simply completed the forms as the plaintiff, leaving the house and most of the money to Melissa. Then she completed her part of our no-fault divorce, sent it in to the court, and presto, soon it was done. I wanted to give her most everything because I was pretty sure my monkish lifestyle would not require a lot of money. Also, I wanted to give her the lion's share to help assuage my guilt over leaving her when she was innocent of any wrongdoing.

The Course metaphysics says that I, the Son of God, had the insane idea to separate from God. As soon as I had that thought, I feared God would be angry. I felt terror at his wrath and in an instant made the world, a big illusion in form, as a place to hide from Him. Then I fell asleep in a dream. God, being Spirit, could not enter the world of form. So, I would continue my dream life in this world of illusion until I woke up to the truth. I couldn't do that until I forgave the illusion. That involved consistently choosing to hear the voice of the Holy Spirit and aligning my thoughts with God's.

As I look back on it, the Course fosters isolation and discourages engagement with the world. All the serious Course students I know have ceased participating in their families, friends, and politics. They have dropped out of the world.

In addition to receiving the guideline from Jesus about no people pleasing, Hoffmeister had announced that he had also received the guideline from Jesus, "no private thoughts." No private thoughts is the ultimate statement of cultic mind control. You will not even *think* differently than the cult leader and *A Course in Miracles*. I don't remember Hoffmeister demanding to know my private thoughts, but he was very clear about what the official line of thinking was in most subjects, such as who could, and who could not, have a relationship. Hoffmeister and his devotees were practicing no people-pleasing so effectively when I was living there that I thought they didn't like me or appreciate me. It was like living alone or in a military environment, without polite forms of address. You just cut straight to the business—edit this, upload that.

Each spirit mind center was managed by one of Hoffmeister's Messengers. The Messengers followed Hoffmeister's will. The Messenger might choose to manage the day-to-day work of the center directly or through a steward. One of the stewards in Utah was fiendishly attached to mundane rules and would call you to account for minor errors such as not washing and drying your laundry at exactly your prescribed hours. At such moments I felt humiliated The strictness was over the top. Even another Messenger referred to it as being like a concentration camp. Later, things loosened up when that steward was replaced. Rule enforcement was more relaxed in the Mexico center. I always worked hard to follow the rules. I wanted enlightenment and the love of God.

Living in this state of withdrawal from society, however, had the effect of diminishing my sense of personal agency, my sense that I was a person who could influence things happening outside of me. The result was that I began to feel weak and less good about myself. Previously, I had been active in politics. And most of all, I had been deeply engaged with my family and friends. Now that was all gone. When I thought about it, I felt like shit. But I still, beyond that, I wanted the love of God.

Because it was mostly an internet ministry, David had a large following scattered around the world. In the fall of 2014, I volunteered to go on David's European tour as the media technician. In Europe, David, some Messengers and I conducted twenty-six multiday retreats and one-day gatherings. We were scheduled in Ireland, Scotland, Finland, Denmark, Holland, Hungary, Spain, Portugal,

Greece, and England. I was very busy setting up cameras, microphones, amplifiers, and mixers before each event. I would film and record David's presentation during and following the event.

The first night I plugged our mixer into a 220-volt European socket and instantly fried it. I was panicked, afraid that this action would ruin the tour and bring wrath down upon me. Fortunately, a kind Irishman named Ian took me on a search all around Dublin and we were able to replace the mixer with the exact same model!

Each night I edited the audio and video and combined them to make a special "Awakening Moment" video and audio. I would then upload them to YouTube and Spreaker, forward the links back to the United States, and archive the edited video. I thought these awakening moments were very exciting, but it seemed like I was sending them into the void. Only later did a European volunteer tell me that she really liked them and looked forward to them every day.

As a volunteer I flew separately, paid my own way, and stayed in cheaper accommodations. It was definitely hierarchical and felt similar to the Hindu caste system. David was the one and only Brahmin, the Messengers were the second tier, and I was down near the bottom, not quite an untouchable. I recognized I was not as attuned to the Holy Spirit as the Messengers on the tour were. However, in Finland, Kyle gave a talk and afterward David reamed him out. David went on and on about what was wrong with Kyle's presentation in front of the rest of us. That marked the end of Kyle's potential career as a Living Miracles presenter.

I remember having a great time walking around in neat little towns in Finland and also visiting Budapest, Hungary, the two countries I hadn't been to before. I was grateful that the people who were supporting us in each country were enthusiastic about David and the Course and fluent in English.

I remember driving in Greece with some Messengers and seeing signs for Macedonia. This triggered my thinking about Alexander the Great and a great biography of him I had read. In the car, I related Alexander's journey from Macedonia and his conquests of Persia, Egypt, and part of India and how he had spread Hellenistic culture through much of the known world. There was no interest in any of this in the car in which I was riding. If it wasn't David or the Course, to them it was nothing but a waste of time. I was happy to return to Mexico and my friend Emma, with whom I could have wider-ranging conversations.

After about a year in Mexico, to my disappointment, it was decided by David and the Messengers that I go to British Columbia, Canada. They tried to keep us moving so we didn't get attached to one spot. Also, they may have thought I was getting too close to Emma. In British Columbia, I would provide training to people interested in learning more about the practical application of the Course and about their possibly joining Living Miracles. The center was based in a house with two other guys in the interior of Vancouver Island. This location allowed me to take long walks among huge Douglas fir trees and along a pristine stream for swimming.

Sitting on the large sunny rocks by the stream one afternoon afforded me a good look at one of the other volunteers at the center. She had a nice figure in a bathing suit. I went over to her.

"Isn't this a beautiful spot?" I asked.

"Yes, it is. But actually, I have to get back to do some office work." And she gathered her things and left. She possessed the same remoteness from interpersonal emotional life as other Messenger women, adrift in a metaphysical cloud. I knew she had left her husband and small children behind in Manitoba. One older woman, Margaret, had permanently left her family. She was thriving in the spiritual life and living in community, first in Utah and then in Mexico. Her digestive system was sensitive to many foods, and she introduced me to the nutritional work of Doctor Michael Greger, a rock-solid nutrition scientist, whose work I was to become more deeply involved with.

The Canadian outpost of Living Miracles was headed up by Howard, a former electronics salesman who was a bit of a bully. I was immediately relegated to second place in decisions about food and the physical property. It was at this time that I began leading online zoom discussion groups about David's book *Awakening through A Course in Miracles*. These were a lot of fun for me. The participants spanned several different time zones, which required a bit of planning about our start time. To prepare, I would read the selection for the week and then go online with a few focused discussion questions. Often participants started describing difficult situations they were facing in their lives, and I became as much a spiritual counselor as a book discussion leader. I continued to lead this online discussion group for a few years, regardless of where I was living. We also organized and conducted several small ACIM discussion gatherings in Victoria. During these, Howard took second place.

Then the opportunity arose for Howard and me to teach a multiday retreat to a group of experienced course students in Calgary, Alberta. Howard and I had a scenic trip through the Canadian Rockies. We drove by stunning forested mountains and pristine blue lakes along the way culminating in Banff National Park. Then we drove on to Calgary.

During the first morning at the retreat center, I led the group of about twelve on an intellectual summation of the Course metaphysics. In the afternoon two participants asked me questions about how I personally handled relationships. I found a certain resentment coming up in my mind about the Course's position on special relationships and David's emphasis on no people- pleasing. I felt these concepts had handicapped me, made it impossible for me to have satisfying love relationships or friendship relationships in the community. I felt I always had to be neutral and treat everyone the same way. So, I retreated to metaphysics when these questions came along, which was unsatisfying for the participants (and for me).

Howard seized the opportunity. Although I thought he spoke rather simplistically, getting the metaphysics a little backward, he was speaking from his heart. And the audience warmed to him. They began talking about their interpersonal relationships, which used to be my communication specialty.

A woman said, "I like to do the dishes right after dinner. The food isn't stuck to the plates and then I have a clean kitchen in the morning. I'd like my husband to help, but it's okay if he doesn't. The problem is he goes into the living room and starts watching a movie on Netflix. Then when I come in, I've missed the whole beginning of the movie. I've asked him to wait for me, but he won't. He just says, 'I'll fill you in about what happened.' This is typical of his selfish behavior. What do I say to him?"

Howard suggested telling him to either start helping with the dishes or to wait until the dishes are done. Others jumped in and it dishes or to wait until the dishes are done. Others jumped in and it became an animated discussion.

But now I felt blocked by the Course and David's no people-pleasing strictures. I felt removed from the group and only added a sentence or two after that.

The next day I just let Howard run with it. I smiled, quoted a bit from the Course, but felt inauthentic and hollow. Howard was having a field day talking off the top of his head.

I realized I was not living what I was teaching. Not only was this retreat a bust for me, but on a higher level, I had realized I had failed to establish a relationship with the Holy Spirit. This saddened me a great deal. It was a soul sickness—I could not walk the talk of David and the Messengers.

After about seven months of kicking around in Canada doing smaller workshops and leading online groups, I was still feeling unsatisfied. I then received an offer to return to the Utah center and flew there.

Back in Utah I proceeded to edit videos all day in the studio, a large windowless room. We had converted a two-story garage into a video and audio studio. We installed special lighting, painted it black and put up lots of sound-catching panels. We also had a green screen so we could fill in behind a speaker with any background we wanted. I had a workstation on the side for video editing.

The Messenger in charge of the studio practiced "no people-pleasing" with a vengeance. She created an oppressive environment where nothing I did was appreciated and I was taken to task if there was any dust to be found on my computer, hard drives, or monitor.

Life under her rule sucked. And another incident of oppression comes to mind.

We got most of our food free from soup kitchens—such things as canned food past its expiration date and stale cakes. The Center said it was a low-income religious household of eleven people in order to be eligible for the free food. I was paying $1000 a month, which didn't square with low income, but many religious orders receive gifts and donations. This free food was supplemented with food from the grocery store. One time Steven was going to the store, and I saw one of the items on his list was apples. A ray of sunshine opened in my mind.

"Great!" I said, "Can you please get any variety of apples except 'delicious' apples? I just don't like their taste."

Steven heard me with a blank, non-committal face. He returned from the store with, among his other purchases, a bag of *delicious* apples. I don't think his motivation was simply to spite me. But having personal preferences in anything was seen to be of the ego, and hence discouraged. Also, delicious apples were the cheapest, which was a Living Miracles priority.

My complaints only proved to the Messengers that I was spiritually weak and incompetent. Maria, my only friend in the Living Miracles community, suggested that I go on a road trip with Nell, an ACIM-infused country singer. I thought Maria must have insight into what I needed, and I was eager to get out of the oppressive studio.

So, I went on the tour with singer Nell, starting at the Peacehouse in Cincinnati and traveling through North Carolina, Georgia, and Florida. The idea was that Nell would sing and I would speak.

But I never spoke. Nell was a hard and loud-spoken woman. It was all about the performance. And, truth be told, I was glad not to speak, as my inner self-confidence was still on the wane.

On the way back we stayed in Durham, North Carolina, with Amanda, and her extended household. Here I discovered a really loving group of four Course people who spoke freely and enjoyed their mutual friendship. I had a great time talking with them over dinner. What a pleasant change. Nell noticed my warming to them but didn't say anything. The following morning, Nell woke me up just before dawn and said, "Come on, we're leaving; pack your bags."

I grabbed everything, loaded the car and she had me drive all the way back to David's old Peacehouse in Cincinnati. During the ride, Nell told me that I was wrong to talk with people outside David's Living Miracles community so openly. She said it looked like a sign I was thinking of leaving the community. Nell said she had emailed this information about me to Messenger Alice. *What? Nell was reporting my actions?*

That night I pulled the car into the long Peacehouse driveway. Then Nell told me she had just received an email from Alice threatening me with being thrown out of the community unless I restated my allegiance. I was smacked by this letter. I stood there shaking. Then Nell told me to drive to Paula's house in Cincinnati. I began backing down the long dark driveway. There were no lights. I backed into the blackness of the street and banged into a car parked on the far side. The impact dented the other car and broke the taillight on David's car.

Nell immediately called to report me to the Messengers, who were furious. Nell said that the Messengers said I couldn't leave

Cincinnati until I paid the other car owner off, because David didn't have insurance. (This was a lie because David did have insurance. It was an Ohio state law that everyone had to have collision insurance.) I had the taillight replaced the next day, but the other driver wouldn't go along with the payoff because his friends had advised him to follow the regular insurance channels.

Alice reiterated that I couldn't come back to the center until I had paid off the expenses of repairing the other guy's car. I was reeling, traumatized, felt I was thrown out of heaven, like a large blunt object had hit me hard on the side of the head. A black wind was rushing through my mind. My world was being tossed up and away. Communications like this originated with David and were transmitted by the Messengers. The Messengers were simply his mouthpieces. There was no appeal.

I hadn't really done anything seriously wrong but felt condemned nonetheless because the source was Living Miracles. I was a failure before God and man. They told me I couldn't fly back to the center. Nell flew back. I stayed but couldn't sleep.

Then, finally, the next day I got word that I could fly back. When I flew back to the Living Miracles Center, nobody greeted me. I went back into the windowless studio and recommenced editing videos all day. They stopped asking me to drive runs to and from the Salt Lake airport to pick people up and drop people off. I was blacklisted for driving. I let my license expire. I was internalizing their negative judgments of me. I became seriously depressed. I was dejected and miserable. When I moved, I went like an automaton.

By winter I was in such bad shape I felt I was going to lose my mind. I experienced a constant low-grade dizziness, spaciness. I was desperate. I implored the Messengers to let me fly back down to Mexico to their new Wellness Center in Chapala, so that I might be in a nurturing environment. They, probably having asked David, agreed to let me go. Mexico had been the site of some of my happiest Living Miracles memories. Living Miracles was boasting about their new wellness accommodation (David's unused room) along with a restorative program of centering, meditation, fresh food, and sunshine.

But when I got there, I was put in a no-frills room. Emma, unfortunately, was back in Australia. The only wellness aspect was that I was alone in a room and not in the bunk room. All I could do was sit and stare. I went back on antidepressants. Things went from bad to worse. Messenger Charlotte decided I needed to have my ego dismantled further. I was put in a room in an outbuilding that was off by itself, not a bedroom. It was a hike across the quadrangle to get to the bathroom. I was relegated to sweeping the walks, chopping vegetables, and vacuuming the pool. I felt completely washed out.

I was so down no one wanted to talk to me. I had requested that a volunteer come to my room every morning so we could read and discuss the daily lesson from the Course workbook. I kept trying to absorb the lesson and live it, but it had no traction. The lessons seemed completely abstract. I would raise objections or ask difficult questions about the lesson's application. One after the other, each volunteer would get sick of working with me, and another one would volunteer. I felt like an untouchable.

With the exception of Esther. She had recently married Kyle. But where Kyle was hard, she was soft. Where he was all business, she was kind. She agreed to meet with me every morning to do a

Course lesson and discuss it. Where I had depression, she had joy. She was a beautiful singer, classically trained. I loved hearing her sing "A Thousand Years," at a gathering. I also remember watching her dancing happily to some Mexican folk music. Yet, even with her I was largely unresponsive. I felt stuck.

I had nowhere else to go. In the last call I had had with my sister, many months ago, she didn't encourage me in any way to leave and come back to Massachusetts. She did say she had health issues. Not a promising escape for me. I thought about Jessie and that we had become good friends in Majorca. But she was with a guy now, maybe even married. I was ashamed of how I'd left Melissa. I had divorced her by mail. I had lost touch with Evan. I didn't want to return there in total defeat. I couldn't really drop in on former Living Miracles folks and expect a warm welcome. I had pretty much avoided each of them after they left. Maybe visit Mateo in Guatemala? What an imposition I would be. Maybe he hardly remembered me. I couldn't imagine just setting out on my own. I didn't feel able to get a job. I wished I were dead.

One stormy night I sneaked out of the outbuilding and, in the rain, cut myself a length of rope from the rope the gardener had been using to tie up a leaning banana tree. I cut off enough to make a sufficiently long hanging rope. I studied all manner of ways to commit suicide. I just wanted to end my life.

Over the next few weeks, I spent a fair amount of time looking around the property for a spot to hang myself, like the shower; not high enough. Some projections were high enough and strong enough, but they were all too visible within the little Living Miracles compound. Someone might come by and interrupt.

During the day, I was allotted the task of walking a stray dog, Benito, one of the Messengers had taken in. As I walked through town, I checked out all the high spots from which I might hang myself with a sufficient drop. Surprisingly few were both high enough and accessible. Accessibility was difficult because all the properties in this part of Chapala were surrounded by eight-foot walls to prevent people from stealing stuff.

On one of my walks, I crossed over a small stone bridge with just a trickle of water going under it in the dry season. I thought I might secure a rope on the bridge and jump off it. I looked over the edge and saw a dead shepherd-like dog with flies on him and a bunch of trash. It was fitting for my macabre mood, but too busy with traffic.

In the community I was no longer able to perform higher tasks. I couldn't concentrate to read, certainly couldn't edit writing, videos, or audios. I could see that I had lost a good deal of my cognitive function, couldn't do things the others could do.

Yet somehow, as a little glimmer in my mind, I thought that this could still be my path. That I needed this big lesson in humility and the dismantling of my ego as a kind of cleansing of my soul. All I needed to do was stick it out, stay on David's bus, and a miracle would happen. I would experience a complete transformation in the end. It was my only shot. But in my gut, I feared this last shot was a lost cause.

Kyle showed us, maybe ten people, a movie about Jesus and Judas. There was quite a discussion about Judas and what was going on in his mind when he betrayed Jesus. Did Judas really understand Jesus's spiritual role, or was he focused on making the best temporal use of Jesus abilities? Fear came over me. I felt like I was secretly

Judas, the disbeliever, hiding my nonbeliever attitude. I didn't want to be found out.

I determined that I absolutely had to leave the community, even escape Mexico. I decided to head for the Guadalajara airport. But I knew they were watching me closely. I developed a plan. I called our usual cab driver to take me to a doctor's appointment in the late morning. I packed all my bags, including my hanging rope. Then I took my suitcases to the side entrance of the community and buzzed the gate open. No one was watching as I put my suitcases in the trunk of the cab. Then I went around to the main entrance and got in the cab in plain sight. Instead of the doctor's office, I told the driver to take me to the airport and I checked into the airport Hampton Inn. Lying on the bed I reflected that I didn't know what to do next.

I had read up on hanging to death. In a long-drop hanging the force of the falling body is sufficient to break the neck and tear the spinal column thus causing immediate brain death. The short-drop hanging is slower, but if done correctly, the tightening noose causes asphyxiation and cuts off the blood circulation from the carotid artery to the brain. I had gone over the process several times, and all I needed was a solid 6½-foot door. I would tie the rope to the doorknob on the far side of the door and throw the rope over such that the noose hung near the top on the near side. The closet door in the room met the specifications. But I was afraid that I might be pursued and didn't want to be interrupted.

The phone rang. *That must be the Messengers!* The cab driver had probably been questioned by the Messengers and had told them that he had taken me to the hotel and not the doctor. I suspected the

Messengers would come to get me. So I hurriedly repacked my stuff, checked out of the Hampton Inn, and jumped into the airport shuttle bus that was around the corner. Sure enough, I saw Charlotte and Nell pull up in front of the hotel, go in, and return in frustration to their car. I crouched low in the shuttle bus. I felt like I was in a thriller movie. They left.

I took the shuttle through the airport to a nearby Mexican hotel, got out and checked in. The lobby was decorated with a lot of shiny black and clear plastic shapes on the wall. I went to my room and the same black motif carried through. *How appropriate,* I thought. I made sure the door was locked. The measurement of the closet door was right for my short-drop hanging. I decided now was the time to hang myself. I had no excuse not to.

I opened the closet door. It was dark inside. Suddenly I was overcome by a wave of fear, of blackness, of deep terror. The strongest panic I had ever experienced. I realized *Oh my God I don't want to kill myself! I'm afraid to die! Anything but this! My fate is not to die in some lousy Mexican hotel.* I shut the closet door, and I paused to enjoy my breathing. After a while my heartbeat settled down.

I had failed to kill myself. What to do next? Planes were available, but I had no place to fly to, didn't know a friend I could see. All my bridges were burned a long time ago.

In my failure I had one resort. I called tough-minded Charlotte at Living Miracles. She said to take a taxi back to the Living Miracles Center, which I did. I walked into the brick-and-tile kitchen. Everyone knew what had happened, but no one even made eye contact, much less asked me how I was or welcomed me back. But actually, I was glad to be alive.

And my life groaned on. As the weeks passed, the one thing that was even slightly positive was getting up early and talking with Messenger Sophia during her early-morning cigarette. Sophia was in charge in Mexico. She was short, a bit overweight and energetic. I would pass through a courtyard, climb up a set of external, fire escape-type stairs and find her taking periodic, long, slow inhales of her cigarette, holding it, and blowing the smoke out. I would sit next to her, and she would ask, "How's it going?" I would quite frankly lay out what was going on with me, my latest upset or complaint, and she would engage me in conversation. She didn't try to fix me, but she was a good person to talk to.

One day at the Living Miracles Center Mexico community, I was surprised to learn I had inherited a lot of money from my deceased mother. Her mother, my grandmother, had held stock in Woolrich Woolen Mills. The company had been doing badly when, by a stroke of luck, it was purchased by an Italian clothing company. My gain was $225,000 which had come to the Living Miracles Center in Utah as a check in the name of my revocable trust. Trouble was I would have to return to the US to get a medallion signature guarantee in order to get the money out of the trust.

How might I use this money? For freedom? I felt I couldn't leave the community because I still had nowhere to go. I had burned all my bridges with family. Divorced my wife. Sold, given away, or trashed everything I owned.

No, I could afford to pay my $1,000 a month and just stay where I was for a while longer. Maybe that Mexican doctor I'd seen a few times who was pushing ketamine therapy could fix me. Ketamine was still an experimental treatment for depression, but the look of his office didn't inspire confidence. I was wary of the psychedelic aspect of ketamine, as my brother had warned me not to take psychotropic drugs, and I didn't have a support person. Forget that.

Then David sent me an ultimatum through his Messenger, Sophia. I either pay Living Miracles $225,000 or leave the community!

This was outrageous, I protested! This was the antithesis of love. This was blatant coercion. David knew what bad shape I was in. Now he was going to take my money or kick me out. *That bastard! That hypocrite! Preaching love to others and ripping me off.*

I was desperate. I didn't want to crawl off and die, even with the money. My mind flashed on the dead dog under the bridge. Sophia was really all the community I had. They'd given me a better place to sleep in the Living Miracles compound. Mexico was a nice country. I didn't want to be completely alone. Maybe David was right about getting the earthly temptation of money out of my way.

I had a day to think about it. I went out and paced for a long time in the streets of Chapala. The cobblestone streets and sidewalks were in major disrepair, so I had to watch where I stepped as I agonized over this choice. If I kept the money and took off, would I be comfortable checking into a hotel someplace? Probably not. Flying somewhere? Where? No, I needed the company of people I knew, some kind of social network. Damn. If only I hadn't broken off so definitively with Melissa and Evan, with my sister. She hadn't contacted me except once to say her husband was having an operation. I was really alone.

Staying with Living Miracles would at least give me a group of people I knew, and at best a chance at awakening to my higher self. Although this had begun to appear to be a very long shot.

So, the next day I told the Messengers I'd give them the money. Sophia was surprised that that was my decision. I suspect that she didn't fully approve of David's ultimatum, but she didn't let on. After a brief hesitation, she said she was glad I'd chosen to stay. I figured I could at least live my life out as a scurvy dog in this little compound in Chapala.

My life seemed to have a huge aspect of unreality. I felt I was sleepwalking, or an astronaut who'd lost his tether to the ship and was floating endlessly off into the darkness of space. Plane reservations were made to get me to the United States so I could get the funds and then transfer them.

I flew to Las Vegas with Sophia to obtain the medallion signature guarantee in a US bank, the essential step in getting the money. We stayed in a casino that was a short distance off the strip. Walking through the first floor of the casino was a major assault on the senses: lights, beeps, and bells, rows of people pulling the arms of slot machines, scantily clad bar girls offering drinks to the gamblers. I saw one skinny older lady with long white hair and a laundry basket full of quarters, mechanically feeding a machine and compulsively pulling the lever.

After we checked into our room, Sophia asked me for money, and I gave her $120 in cash. Heck, she was a Messenger, and I was giving all my money to Living Miracles. Sophia gambled for about six hours and lost almost all the money I had given her. Casinos were not new to her. As we were walking out, she had a few dollars left in a casino ticket voucher. She gave it to me. I put it in a slot machine, pulled the handle and won $1200! Lights flashed and bells went off. Sophia claimed that it was her money I used in the machine, hence the $1200 was all hers. We argued, and eventually she settled for half. I bought a long-sleeve shirt because I didn't have one.

We went to the bank the next morning. Armed with the bank's medallion signature guarantee, I flew to Utah to transfer the $225,000 to Living Miracles, but also to consult with Maria, the only person I still trusted in the Living Miracles ministry. The place was so familiar. In her large bedroom we lay on her bed together and thought it over. Maria told me, yes, it was good for my connection with the Holy Spirit to give the money to Living Miracles. She also said that I should continue to give money, $1000 a month extra, to free me spiritually. The next day she accompanied me to the bank to transfer the $225,000. Over the next six months I gave an additional $1,000 a month, per her request. I didn't feel good about it, but I trusted her.

I stayed in Utah with just my one suitcase and my laptop. I didn't want to go back to Mexico to get the rest of my stuff. Kamas was okay and my friend Maria was here. Maria occasionally had me edit her emails for correct English, but after a couple of months, she seemed to lose interest in me. The Messengers in Kamas had a separate luxurious wing of the building. Not hearing from Maria, I began to suspect giving the money had not been about my spiritual growth. One day she informed me that David had bought a temple on a hill in Mexico overlooking Chapala. *With my money*, I thought. *That egotistical hypocrite.*

At the Kamas Living Miracles Center I mowed the lawn, pruned the hedges, and watered the flowers on the borders and in the window boxes. I also maintained the hot tub, checking the chemicals and cleaning it. Inside the large French Provincial-style house, I did some vacuuming and cleaning of the men's bunk and bathroom. I edited videos in the garage that had been turned into a studio. Sometimes I helped out video recording David or one of the Messengers. It wasn't much of a life.

It was in August when, early in the morning, Messenger Janet came into the volunteers' dining area, pulled out a chair and sat next to me.

"Andy, we are done talking to you."

"What?

"No one will talk to you anymore."

"No one?"

"That's it." She held my gaze. Then she got up.

Wow! I would, in effect, be getting the silent treatment. *My God, this is clear proof that they hate me! Let me out of here!* I felt slightly dizzy. This was definitely the end. I went to pack my stuff. When I encountered Maria at the door of the men's bunkroom, she was looking at me as if I were an object, not a human being. I really wanted a smile and a hug. But her tone was cold and matter-of-fact as she asked me for the pesos for the others' taxi money.

It hit me hard, to be so depersonalized by someone I had loved—the only person I had trusted in the end at Living Miracles Center. I internalized it. I felt that I was unlovable as a person and a spiritual failure. I was the one who couldn't succeed spiritually where all the others had succeeded. I forgot about all those who had left Living Miracles Center over the years. I had seen them as dropouts, people who were not going to experience the spiritual awakening that those of us who stayed would surely attain. I had even thought of it as riding on the Course in Miracles bus, driven into heaven by David, the only Course teacher who was actually living the Course.

Now, I didn't know where to go.

For me to leave would prove that I had been completely, devastatingly wrong. Wrong to leave Melissa and my family. Wrong in the eyes of everyone who knew me, in the spiritual community and outside it. Wrong in the eyes of David, the prophet who was leading people to the true love of God. And finally, wrong in the eyes of God, who must have decided I just didn't mea-sure up, wasn't to be enlightened, awakened, or loved, but was rather a shallow ego, a complete failure with no place to go.

Now I just wanted to get out of the Living Miracles Center. There was less than nothing here for me. Fuck them.

12.

Escape With My Son's Help

Then I remembered I still had to get my laptop and a flicker of hope came into my mind. I went into the windowless studio to fetch it. The room was empty. I had left my laptop on the desk, and I opened it eagerly. Yes, there was the email letter from my son, Evan, that I hadn't given full attention because I was following the rule of not communicating with friends and family. I sat down. It read:

Hi Dad,

I want to express the impact that your being away is for me. I don't just miss you – in the way that someone might miss a person that was on a long vacation – I am scared, honestly, that I might not see you again.

That's scary for me too, I thought.

There's a person that I know named Andrew LeCompte, someone who was my guide and role model, the person I looked up to every day of my childhood and young adult life. That's a real thing for me. And you are very real to me. I don't want to pretend anymore that your absence is not having a *profound* impact on me.

You have my attention.

There was a day when I was about 12 years old when you handed me a copy of *A Course in Miracles*, saying it was like the 'Bible' for our family. Truth be told, I liked that idea a great deal. A spiritual solidarity, in written words, that you and I, could rely on when happiness was not present. Through the years, you related to me many of the teachings and insights you had gained through your study of ACIM. At times, we discussed in an intellectual way, the core ideas of the book. When your devotion to the Course seemed to take on a new level after you had edited Hoffmeister's book, I was happy for you, and I thought that David must be a very enlightened man. I support what you are doing, your spiritual journey, your calling.

Wow, he supports me. I don't even support myself.

But why does your spiritual journey need to exclude your family? I *love* you and *care* for you deeply.

I love you too!

Your spiritual awakening is one that I am very much in support of. At the same time, I see the possibility of your spiritual awakening coinciding with your love and connectedness with your family. Your connection with the God of your understanding, and that connection being all the more real by us connecting with you and being part of a miracle of human transcendence.

I would love nothing more than to be a part of your awakening. I want to be part of your life, and I have been afraid to say that for the 6-odd years that you've been away.

179

I'm ashamed that I haven't had an awakening.

I've been afraid that you might say something or do something that would somehow leave me in absence of you forever.

Will you let me be part of your life again?

When can I see you? When can we talk on the phone? You have my number.

> With love,
>
> Evan

Yes, I so much want to have you part of my life again! Yes! Yes! Yes!

I read this loving appeal from my son, and the dark veil that had been over my eyes lifted. He didn't hate me. He still loved me and wanted to connect with me. He respected me, even my pursuit of a calling. Tears came to my eyes.

I paused to consider the power of his words. How *could* I, a loving spiritual person exclude love of family, exclude the love of a son for his father? A path that would do such violence to love could not be a true path. That initial requirement that David had demanded of me, that I leave my friends and family in order to be spiritually whole, was a lie. It was the essence of separation, of judging others as not up to a certain spiritual standard. Instead of immersing in a loving community, I ended up living in isolation surrounded by unloving people. I was only kept around for my money. When the money had been coerced out of me, I was expelled and shunned. I had run the complete gamut, from being "love bombed" in the beginning to being given the silent treatment at the end. And now it was done.

On my laptop, I checked out the flights from Salt Lake to Boston. I was able to book a direct flight on United later in the day.

Elated, I called Evan, and he picked up.

"I love you, Evan. I love you *so* much and I'm coming home."

"That's wonderful Dad. I love you too. I'm so glad to hear that. My girlfriend and I will meet you at the airport."

Wow, I was filled with a happy feeling of love and joy. *I have a place to go. My son still loves me, after six long years.* This was the complete reverse of how I was feeling the last time I went to an airport.

A half hour later, I heard the happy tap of the Uber's horn and was off.

On the plane to Boston, I reflected on how Evan and I had had a great relationship when he was a child. We particularly enjoyed swimming and sailing at Sampson Pond in the Adirondacks. Then in late adolescence he had become a heroin addict in Manchester. I had tried all sorts of things to help him, and nothing worked. I didn't know what to do with him. It was during this time that I (thought I) heard the word of God calling me to Utah. So, I went. Evan had resented me for abandoning him, but he had kicked his addiction by staying cold turkey at his mother's house. He was in better shape than I was.

In Boston Evan and his girlfriend picked me up at the airport. It was great to see him! Evan and I had a big hug. He was a couple inches taller than me, lean, strong, and smiling. We drove into Cambridge and Evan said he'd like to take me kayaking on the Charles

River. It was a beautiful windy afternoon with a deep-blue sky. With the Boston skyline on one side and Cambridge on the other I experienced a sense of familiarity and home. It was exhilarating out on the water, fighting the wind, digging my kayak paddle in deeply on both sides, feeling the cold spray, following my son. I finally was free.

I stayed at my sister Anne's house. She welcomed me warmly yet looked at me a bit warily from time to time. I learned that back in the early spring of 2017, she had invited Dr. Steven Hassan, widely known cult expert, to meetings of the whole family at her house. This included her husband, my son, his partner, my nephew and his partner, and my niece and her husband. Apparently, Hassan wanted to find a detective in Mexico who could persuade me to come back. This idea was not followed up on.

My sister told me that I went with the whole family to Bertucci's for pizza, but I've mostly forgotten about this. I was still depressed and, as Anne reported, "hollow."

Six years earlier, I had left my wife and son crying by the side of my driveway and driven off feeling confident that they were not my loving companions, but merely egoic thoughts and temptations. I had given up personal decision-making and my sense of agency in order to follow David Hoffmeister and *A Course in Miracles*. I now see such thinking as insane. I had let David Hoffmeister, his Living Miracles community, and ACIM work on me to bring me to absolute bottom. As I was being kicked out, my son's welcoming letter had saved me. This life-saving miracle occurred on August 8, 2017.

13

Working Through Recovery

I was alive, lying on the bed in my nephew's old bedroom at Anne's house in Lexington, but an empty shell. There was an air conditioner in the window that made a loud noise. There were some clothes hanging off an unused rowing machine. I looked at his childhood bureau and up at the slightly yellowing ceiling light. I was a loser before God and man. I believed I was terminally defective, unable to hear the voice of the Holy Spirit and find God's love. I was also afraid that I could no longer function in the world.

Anne was very solicitous about making me comfortable in her house. We talked a lot in her living room about what I'd been through, what had passed in her family with my niece (now married) and nephew. Also, about me getting health insurance, which I did. I had an upholstered chair that was designated "my" chair. And the food was so much better than in the monastery. She and her husband Bill are terrific cooks.

Wreck that I was, I wanted to learn to think more clearly. Anne had just read *War and Peace*. I had loved it years ago, but when I tried to read it again, I couldn't remember what I'd read a few pages ago. That was a little scary. I put it down.

Anne recommended that I begin seeing a psychiatrist and I went to see a psychiatrist at McLean Hospital. He was a large man with a

Russian accent. Quite formal. He gave me prescriptions for antidepressants which I began taking and we set up a regular schedule of appointments. These visits were primarily medication management. I also signed up for health insurance.

I believed other people saw me as untruthful and of no consequence. After a few weeks I began seeing a psychotherapist to look at and work through issues concerning my posttraumatic stress disorder. My therapist was helpful in believing me and assisting me to begin to see myself as a healthy person who had had some very hard knocks.

Contributing traumas included my being threatened with being thrown out of the community because I had broken David's taillight. I learned that spiritual abuse occurs when a person or group uses spiritual beliefs to hurt, scare, or control you. In this, I believe Living Miracles was a prime offender, denying me any positive feedback under their "no people-pleasing" rule. And then, of course, there was the final trauma of being coerced out of money and then kicked out of the community.

I found some audio programs about enhancing self-esteem and improving brain health and would listen to them on long walks I took from Anne's house. The leaves were beginning to turn bright red and yellow as I walked down the "rail trail," an old commuter railroad line had been paved over to make a smooth pedestrian walkway that had trees on both sides. I didn't have to worry about the whoosh of cars going by, only the mini-whoosh of bicyclers who would call out "on your left" when they were coming up behind me so as not to startle me.

I talked with Anne and my niece about my doing something that would be rehabilitative, make me feel I was helping other people, and that would bring in a little money. My niece, a few years older than Evan and married, came over and was kind and cheerful. She spoke favorably about her experience teaching English as a second language to immigrants. That appealed to me, so I enrolled in a program at the Boston Language Institute for certification as a Teacher of English as a Foreign Language.

I took the bus into Boston every day and did homework for the program every night. It took me a long time to complete the homework assignments, mostly lesson plans and adapting readings that I found on the internet. There was also live practice teaching a group of Chinese immigrants. I was still a bit muddle-brained and made some significant mistakes that I wouldn't have made in the old days, like forgetting to make copies of the handouts! I failed several teaching session milestones. But I kept at it and eventually was able to pass the certification program, although it took me a few weeks longer than my classmates.

Going into Kenmore Square every day I saw a lot of happy couples, many of them hand in hand. They were continual reminders that I wanted to have a "special relationship," the forbidden fruit of ACIM. I talked it over with Anne who was very supportive. My niece spoke favorably about how people she knew were making good relationship connections online. I decided to try it. Wanting to be authentic, I took a selfie of myself in a simple T-shirt at the dining room table. Then I posted it on an online dating service for seniors called Our Time.

I posted the following profile.

A little about me...

I am a pleasant and reliable companion. I like conversation and am able to pay close attention as a listener. I am looking for a long-term relationship with a woman who wants to join and share at a deep level. I like open and honest communication and feeling expression.

I recently returned from living six years in a spiritual community based on *A Course in Miracles*. There I hoped to awaken spiritually. But finally, I found that monastic life just wasn't working for me. So, I returned to New England and am temporarily living at my sister's house in Lexington.

I expect I lost most readers right there. LOL

To balance my profile out a bit I'd like to mention that in 2000 I wrote a book on a topic close to my heart, *Creating Harmonious Relationships: A Practical Guide to the Power of True Empathy*. It was quite successful and sold out. It was even translated into Turkish. From the ideas in the book, I developed the Let's Talk training program, which I taught across the country.

About the one I'm looking for...

Someone who is open and honest, with a sense of humor and hopefully a positive outlook on life, active rather than passive, likes cooking together, likes going out into nature, contra dancing, theater maybe, listening to music (classical, oldies), compassionate, and with other attributes waiting to be discovered. Mass resident.

I'd just like to add...

I inject humor into situations. I do quite well in a group. I like kayaking, hiking, contra dancing, travel, good movies, yoga, and I am getting back into reading.

I really didn't expect much of a response, given that in the first paragraph I had essentially said I was a failed monk, without a job, and living at my sister's.

A woman named Brenda was the first person to respond, however, so I immediately checked out her profile.

A little about me...

I am caring, happy, expressive, and friendly. I know who I am and what I want in life. Life is to be shared and I'm excited about the possibility that another great man just may be out there. I'm very comfortable with people and emotionally mature. I also know that there is always something new to learn about myself and our wonderful world.

About the one I'm looking for...

You're good-natured, energetic, affectionate, and fun. You are "comfortable in your own skin." You're masculine yet gentle and kind. You know what you want, and you are happy. You enjoy music and nature.

I'd just like to add...

I love exploring beautiful little towns and the countryside places like Concord, Groton, Martha's Vineyard, Vermont, and Montreal. I like buying fresh vegetables at local farms and going home to cook them for dinner the same day. I enjoy just staying in at times and appreciating the warmth and comforts of home. I like swimming and sailing.

I also enjoy the activity and excitement of the city (in small doses). I enjoy holding dinner parties and house concerts and hanging out with friends. In recent years I rediscovered the joy of singing and performing and listening to live music by the many talented local musicians around. (I love Blues, Rock, Jazz, Folk, Classical...)

I enjoy being a part of projects that help the community.

I liked that she said she was happy, comfortable with people, and emotionally mature. Also, that she liked music and Montreal.

So, after some email exchanges and a few phone calls we arranged to meet at the Villa Lago restaurant in Lexington. This was a place I could walk to from my sister's house, as I still didn't think I could handle driving a car. My first impression on seeing Brenda was that she had a pretty face and looked Mexican. She had medium-length brown hair. As we began to talk, I could hardly believe how easy it was. She was a great person to talk to and was a lot like me. We quickly discovered that we were both ENFPs on the Myers-Briggs Type Inventory, the enthusiastic, caring, people-centered type.

Back when I was completing my master's program at Associates for Human Resources, I had done an internship at Digital Equipment Corporation under Ben Fordham. Brenda had worked at Digital in human resources and knew Ben Fordham. Small world! I was wondering *What if I'd met her then?* The whole trajectory of my life would have changed for the better.

We talked about everything as we each got happier and happier. Walking back to her car I spontaneously said, "I'd like to kiss you," and we kissed. Then I walked back to my sister's house with a big smile on my face. It was August 23, 2017, The day before my sixty-ninth birthday.

Brenda had been particularly drawn to me as a humanist and an empathic person as demonstrated in my book. I liked that, because that was who I really was, not the more aloof student of ACIM who thought he, and not others, was on the one true path.

We dated, taking long walks in the woods, and got to know and appreciate each other even more. Although I was still depressed, Brenda didn't notice. She said, "I see you," and part of me believed that she could actually see the real me when I wasn't so sure about myself.

At first, we walked through the town forests in Weston, which are extensive, many with towering white pines and trails cushioned with pine needles. I love to walk in a hushed forest and hear the bird calls and chipmunk rustlings. These walks gave us plenty of time to talk and get to know each other. I used the All-Trails app on my phone, and we never had to do the same walk twice.

One day when we were setting out for a reggae concert in the western part of the state, she handed me the keys and said "Here, you drive." I had gotten a Massachusetts license and I just said "Okay," got into the driver's seat, and away we went. Brenda had prepared a nice little picnic with sushi for us. We did a little dancing to the live reggae music and had a relaxed time lying on a blanket and talking. I was continuously impressed by how genuinely attentive she was to me.

Back at Anne's house, I wondered if the connection had been similar with Melissa. I thought about Melissa. I felt guilty for having left her. I noticed I didn't feel a strong impulse to connect with her, but I wasn't feeling much in the way of strong impulses for anything. I had a lot of respect for Melissa and wanted to find out what she was thinking about our relationship after these six years.

So, I called her, and she invited me to come up. I drove to Dover,

New Hampshire, saw her apartment, and spent an afternoon walking and talking with her. She had two cute little cats. She was glad to see me, and she indicated she would like me to decide if I wanted to start up our relationship again. I noticed I didn't like her perfume and that that strongly influenced my impression. I was annoyed with myself that I let such a trivial thing influence me. I wanted to right the wrong I had done to her. Yet maybe my inner voice was telling me it was time to move on.

So, I called her, and she invited me to come up. I drove to Dover, New Hampshire, saw her apartment, and spent an afternoon walking and talking with her. She had two cute little cats. She was glad to see me, and she indicated she would like me to decide if I wanted to start up our relationship again. I noticed I didn't like her perfume and that that strongly influenced my impression. I was annoyed with myself that I let such a trivial thing influence me. I wanted to right the wrong I had done to her. Yet maybe my inner voice was telling me it was time to move on.

I came home and talked with Anne about my not knowing what to do about Melissa and Brenda. I felt I needed to make a choice. Anne thought Brenda was better for my mental health and meeting my current needs. I thought so too. Anne thought that I had to make a decision now. I decided on Brenda and sent an email to Melissa saying I was no longer in love with her. I didn't want it to be hurtful but knew it would be. More guilt. I felt like a sleazeball.

Now I needed to take care of my mental health. My psychiatrist recommended that I enroll in the Behavioral Health Program at McLean Hospital. I was resistant to McLean Hospital because my older brother, Tony, had been incarcerated there for several months a few years before his suicide. I had to see him with a guard in the room. We couldn't make much of a connection there. I had a *One Flew Over the Cuckoo's Nest* fear of mental hospitals. My sister and her psychiatrist assured me that the hospital had improved a great deal since then. I could see that I really needed a strong and comprehensive program like the Behavioral Health program in order to really recover. So, I got my courage up and enrolled. I was ready to accept psychological help.

One of the first things I did was go to see the program psychiatrist. She was personable and easygoing, in contrast to the formality of my psychiatrist. The quality of her voice was kind, yet firm. I felt I could trust her and expressed what a wreck I was and that I had lost a lot of my cognitive function.

She said, "I don't believe it. Take this test." And she handed me a pencil. I took the test to demonstrate my inability to her, but the test wasn't that hard. She scored it and said I had an almost-perfect score, had scored higher than she had and in a faster time. What a relief! I wasn't crazy! Thank you! Part of my depression seemed to lift right then. My brain was okay.

Over the next ten days at McLean's Behavioral Health Program, I went on to participate in classes in cognitive behavior therapy (CBT), dialectical behavior therapy (DBT), and acceptance and commitment therapy (ACT). The programs consisted of talks and short exercises. I was tired of avoiding looking at myself and feeling less than everyone else. CBT helped me become aware of inaccurate and negative thinking so I could view challenging situations more clearly and respond to them in a more effective way. DBT helped me identify and change suicidal ideation if it were to crop up again. It also reintroduced me to the practice of mindfulness. ACT showed me that my emotions were normal and that I could change them with practice. I took a lot of notes and did the recommended exercises at home.

Yet I still carried in mind the conviction that I had failed to connect with God/the Holy Spirit. I also felt sad and angry about the people in the Living Miracles community, that I had failed to live happily with them and was hence unlovable. My self-talk had one repeated phrase: that I was a failure before God and man.

In the Behavioral Health Program, I identified "I am a failure before God and man" as my primary negative automatic thought (NAT). I was telling myself that I couldn't make it. That I failed God. That God didn't choose me; He chose the others. That I was unlovable, not spiritual, a hypocrite. I didn't love God. I was angry at the Living Miracles community and sorry I had given them all that money.

I listed my feelings about these thoughts: shame, guilt, sadness, anger at being coerced, hopelessness.

This NAT was ingrained, hard to let go of, and influenced my feelings and behavior. It came from never having had the mystical experience of hearing the voice of the Holy Spirit and from never being acknowledged as a positive contributor at Living Miracles Center. How ironic, I sought for years wanting to hear the inner voice of God. Now, in recovery, I was struggling with too much inner voice, now a negative voice, implanted by Living Miracles.

As I thought about my experience at Living Miracles, it became more and more clear that the Living Miracles community was not a loving place but rather the capital of No People-Pleasing. They did not even see people as people, but as thoughts. The community did not practice "love your brother," as Jesus had.

I had worked for David as a volunteer to promote his message for six years, but he had given up on me. The community took from me but never gave back. I lost my voice, actually had trouble talking for a while, was depressed and suicidal. They did not see me as a person. Janet, on the part of the community, condemned me to the silent treatment. David coerced me out of $225,000. Maria Hernandez had pressured an additional $6,000 out of me, was angry at me when I left, and even hit me up for some pesos.

I found adaptive/believable thoughts to replace the NAT: "God is love. I am a loving compassionate person. There are people who love me. I love Evan and Anne and they love me. Brenda loves me and I love Brenda." And this was believable and true. Brenda had moved from saying "I see who you really are" to saying, "I love you." For the first time in my life, I had the feeling of being truly and deeply loved, perhaps because I felt I deserved this love. Brenda was genuinely and consistently loving.

I think that God, after seeing me pursue miracles down a blind alley, decided to give me the real thing—a miraculous special relationship. Almost as soon as I arrived in Massachusetts, I had felt compelled to go online and look. For her part, Brenda had been looking for a loving special relationship for six years, since her first husband died six years before.

I had read on the internet that Mexicans had a happiness gene that made them statistically happier than people without the gene. It may not be entirely true, but I liked it. The country with the highest happiness rating, Mexico, also had the highest estimated prevalence of this "allele," the researchers found. Being sometimes depressed myself, I wanted to marry a Mexican woman. So, while the relationship hadn't happened in Mexico, I was certain that Brenda carried this gene. She admitted that she is happy all the time and her two good friends, Marte and Phyllis, both said that Brenda was exceptional in this regard. Always kind, loving and happy.

When I was feeling stronger, and with Brenda's support, I wrote a formal letter to David Hoffmeister demanding the $231,000 he and Maria had coerced out of me. I sent it certified mail to the Living Miracles Centers in Utah and Mexico and copied the letter to my attorney, stating that if Hoffmeister did not return the money, I would sue him for that amount, plus damages. I had the intention, if he didn't agree, to find the most aggressive anti-cult lawyer in the United States. Then I would sue him, Maria and Living Miracles Center for the money plus a huge amount in psychological damages.

I was mobilized and excited by taking this action. I eagerly awaited his response. I wanted to get the money back so I could support myself. Also, I was thinking if he tried to blow me off, I could let my anger at him have full sway. I was looking for an opportunity to punish his smug ass.

David agreed to all my demands. (Picture me doing a little dance.) I believe he felt he had to return the funds, not so much to be fair, but because I threatened to sue for damages in addition to the $231,000. He sent the money. I breathed a sigh of relief about my financial situation. It also felt like my mind became stronger, no longer intimidated. Yes, I could accomplish things for myself in the world.

Also, I realized my jaw was no longer tense. I took out my night guard and threw it away. No more clenching or grinding. I saw this as a bodily manifestation of my true inner peace.

I had done some writing during the Behavioral Health Program and found it therapeutic. I realized that writing down my experiences about David and Living Miracles could both help me get control of and heal my mind. I could also use writing to alert others to avoid the path I had gone down.

14.

What Makes a Cult

From my new mentally healthy position, I wanted to alert others to the dangers of getting involved with a cult. To prepare for this, I did some research on cults.

Here is the comprehensive definition of a cult from the *Cultic Studies Journal*.

A group or movement exhibiting great or excessive devotion or dedication to some person, idea, or thing, and employing unethical manipulative or coercive techniques of persuasion and control e.g., isolation from former friends and family, debilitation, use of special methods to heighten suggestibility and subservience, powerful group pressures, information management, suspension of individuality or critical judgment, promotion of total dependency on the group and fear of leaving it, designed to advance the goals of the group's leaders, to the actual or possible detriment of members, their families, or the community. (West, L. J., & Langone, M. D. 1986. "Cultism: A conference for scholars and policy makers." Cultic Studies Journal, 3, 119–120.)

I believe David Hoffmeister's Living Miracles community, based on *A Course in Miracles*, neatly fits this definition of a cult.

A Course in Miracles cannot be a cult in and of itself. *A Course in Miracles* is simply a theological book. A cult really needs leadership that is manipulative or coercive. ACIM does not have an official organization or leader. Its 365-lesson workbook is expressly to be self-taught, a lesson a day. The practice of ACIM, however, more or less subtly, prepares its students to be cult ready. David Hoffmeister capitalized on this cult-readiness of ACIM students when he formed the Living Miracles community.

The Course says that there are two realms, the realm of God's knowledge which is truth and eternity, and the world of perception which consists of interpretations, illusions, scarcity, loss, separation, and death. We humans live and think in the world of perception and our only way out is through forgiveness, in which we recognize our perceptual errors and look past them to our true self that God created. In other words, we on Earth know nothing and need to learn the truth through practicing the Course and/or from a Course teacher.

I shared my process of becoming cult-ready in previous chapters on how I brainwashed myself over decades of devoted study. It had finally come to the point where I doubted my thoughts anytime they seemed to conflict with what I read in the Course. Since the Course said there was no physical world, only projections of spirit/mind, and that the voice of the Holy Spirit was the only truth, I was in pretty much in constant self-doubt.

The Course claims to be the voice of Jesus and a path to the peace of God, hence it has divine authority. It also claims that it is a "required course," implying that each person must eventually come around to taking it. It is a challenging course, a 1,200-page program in mind training with a lesson for each day of the year. The introduction says: "Nothing real can be threatened, Nothing unreal exists, Herein lies the peace of God." It's saying that what's in the Course equates to what is real. There was comfort here for me, that once I knew what was real, I'd have a sort of mental/spiritual invulnerability, an all-knowingness.

The Course states that other people are merely fearful thoughts to be transcended. "He [the student] must become willing to reverse his thinking, and to understand that what he thought projected its effects on him were made by his projections on the world. The world he sees does therefore not exist." Whoa! This is a 100 percent shift in reality. I am responsible for projecting the world! The student gradually retrains his mind to believe in an alternate reality where mind is the only cause. I liked the power of this position, that once I established proper control over my mind, I could establish control over my world, in a loving way.

To "gaslight" means to manipulate someone by psychological means into questioning their own sanity. I became convinced, through immersion in Living Miracles that the Course was the one set of ideas I would ever need. I stopped my regular attendance at meetings of Alcoholics Anonymous and stopped going to the Unitarian Universalist Church on Sundays. I left my friends and family. I studied the Course and meditated on it every day. I gaslighted myself and became insane relative to the real world.

A cult has a central leader. All the money, both given by volunteers who paid $1,000 per month to live there, and by donors, was funneled up to David Hoffmeister. He had special food, luxurious accommodation, and money to travel. David had a large budget to publish books and promulgate his ideas. Living Miracles built many websites, both paid subscription and free, featuring David's video talks. He had an audio channel. He traveled extensively. He also always had a sex partner. All major decisions were made by David and delivered by his Messengers. Yet always, deep down, I wanted David's approval. I no longer had family or friends. I had staked it all on David, believing he had the truth.

Relating back to the definition: In my eyes David Hoffmeister and the Messengers manipulated the truth. For example, I was lied to by the Messenger Alice, who told me that David had no car insurance. She also angrily told me that I couldn't return to the community until I paid off the parties to my car accident. This was traumatizing.

According to ACIM, love relationships and close friendships are deemed "special relationships," which are ego devices that keep the student away from God's plan. This discouraging of personal relationships keeps the student dependent on Course leaders and Course groups. I was fine with losing friends, being fired from jobs, and having no other spiritual input other than ACIM. Ultimately, at the Messengers request, I accepted severing all connections with my wife, my son, the rest of my family, and my past. I hardened my heart to break with them. Their imploring and tears bounced right off my new Teflon heart. I isolated myself.

The Angel Walk is a "love bombing" technique used at the Living Miracles Center as a very powerful special-influence method. So also is the practice of prolonged eye-gazing. I was rendered susceptible to the belief that all these intimate signs of physical affection were manifestations of the love of God.

Another form of love bombing occurred on those occasions when I was very discouraged and went to the one Messengers. I felt I could always trust Maria. She would invite me to cuddle nonsexually, but intimately with her on the bed. I loved her. Several times she told me I was being held back by my attachment to worldly possessions. As I had no other worldly possessions at this point but money, I offered to help pay for several Living Miracles projects. Maria was feigning love to heighten my suggestibility and subservience, such that I came to see giving $236,000 as a good thing for my spiritual development.

"You are not used to miracle-minded thinking, but you can be trained to think that way. All miracle workers need that kind of training." I filtered everything through the ACIM metaphysics, which left no room for ordinary reality. I stopped watching TV, listening to the radio, and reading newspapers or magazines. I only spoke with other Course students. The only things I read were the twelve hundred pages of ACIM and David's books. I only watched and edited David's videos. Phrases like "I am not my body," "sickness is a defense against the Truth," and "God knows nothing of your pain" led me to a lack of empathy for myself and for others. I came to believe that I was mind, and that if I could just control my thoughts as the Course laid out, I would become enlightened and transcend the body's sickness and death.

I memorized a great many Course lessons and paragraphs which I would call upon whenever I felt stressed or tired or in need of an uplift. Yet all this was in complete opposition to my book on empathic communication. Part of my attraction to this not being a body may have had to do with me wanting to be better than other people.

I had frequently had a critical view of the behavior of others. Unfortunately, this mind-only way of relating allowed me to treat Melissa cruelly.

People conform their thinking to a group's thinking all the time. They do it because they want to fit in and because they think the group is more informed than they are. Cult expert Dr. Steven Hassan says his most important goal in freeing a cult member is to get them to think for themselves. He also introduced me to the "dual identity" model, which describes the split between cult identity and the authentic identity. I had completely taken on a cult identity, which would clinically be named a dissociative disorder The Mayo Clinic reports that dissociative disorders are mental disorders that involve experiencing a disconnection and lack of continuity between thoughts, memories, surroundings, actions, and identity. People with dissociative disorders escape reality in ways that are involuntary and unhealthy and cause problems with functioning in everyday life.

The Course states "there are no private thoughts." It states that what I think are my thoughts are meaningless, are nothing. Yet I unconsciously carry guilt about them because they are attacks on God. Hence my individuality and critical judgment were attacks on God, so I must detach from them. I lost faith in my own critical-thinking ability and felt weak and rather helpless. Consistently being told that my thinking was of the ego, and deferring to those who heard the Holy Spirit, led me to withhold my thoughts. I stopped talking, even lost my physical voice for a while. And this trait endures to this day. I have difficulty speaking up and making myself heard with sufficient volume.

I arrived at the Living Miracles community a confident, eager extrovert. When I left six years later my spirit was broken, and I had become a depressed introvert.

In order to truly understand the nature of *A Course in Miracles* it is essential to know the backstory. The scribe of the Course, Helen Schucman, was a bitter and angry woman. Kenneth Wapnick, author of her biography, *Absence from Felicity*, said of Helen, "I have rarely been in the presence of someone with the degree of criticalness possessed by Helen." She was full of negative judgment.

Even the title of his biography of her, *Absence from Felicity*, tells us a great deal. If felicity means happiness, then absence of felicity means unhappiness. Helen's essence was unhappy. Her personality was strongly aggressive and egocentric. She did not act kindly or lovingly. Rather she was of the mind: "Do what I scribed, not what I do." Helen Schucman, an intellectual, wanted healing of the mind to be done alone and intellectually rather than at a heart level with other people.

According to Wapnick, Helen felt sexually attracted to her colleague, Bill Thetford, who typed up her scribing of the Course. But Bill was homosexual, thwarting her desire to control him sexually. Helen blamed Bill for her misery and their special relationship was characterized by hostility; they would argue throughout the day, developing considerable anger toward each other.

Helen's frustration explains the Course's attack on the special love relationship. The Course devotes nine chapters to describing how the special love relationship is an ego (evil) distraction. Love, in ACIM, is abstract. You don't love a person in a body. You love the abstract spirit they represent.

By contrast, the Jesus of the Bible says, "Love thy neighbor."

And Helen's life did not end in the way one would expect of one favored by Jesus. Father Benedict J. Groeschel, who knew Helen over the years, wrote in his book, *A Still Small Voice* (Ignatius Press 1993), of the "incredible darkness that descended upon Helen Schucman in the last years of her life. This woman who had written so eloquently that suffering really did not exist, spent the last two years of her life in the blackest psychotic depression I have ever witnessed... It was almost frightening to be with her." Groeschel p. 79

Groeschel writes: "As a child, Helen's mother had read the Christian Science writings of Mary Baker Eddy to her. A review of Helen's Course and of the writings of Mrs. Eddy would reveal many similarities about the denial of the reality of suffering. In retrospect, it is my opinion that this Course is a good example of a false revelation." Groeschel p. 80

"*A Course in Miracles* does not represent Helen's own thought or convictions. She could often be angry at the book. She once told me: 'I hate that damned book.'" Groeschel p. 76

"To her great discomfort, with publication of the Course, Helen's identity became known. She was embarrassed and confided to me [Groeschel] her fear that the Course could become a cult. Unfortunately, *A Course in Miracles* has become something of a sophisticated cult, and its followers are caught up in the general wave of Gnosticism that one observes as genuine religious conviction wanes in our society." Groeschel p. 79

The reality of all of life's pains and indignities is denied. "This is very attractive to those who inhabit the glitzy suburbs of modern cities where one avoids squalor and social injustice. Sin and all its hideousness is replaced by this motto: eat, drink and be merry, because tomorrow we can't die but will just pass on to nicer things." Groeschel . 83

Helen, not Jesus, was the author of *A Course in Miracles*. She was socially and emotionally stunted and unhappy. She attempted, with the power of her intellect, to write a profound spiritual text. But her ideas had no love behind them. She exhorted her students, not to love their brother, but to be separate and trust in the theology she invented. It didn't work for her, and it didn't work for me.

My intense experience of *A Course in Miracles*, coupled with the spiritual abuse I felt I received at Living Miracles, was debilitating to my mind. I was deeply affected, even years after I had left the course community. I still liked people and hoped to experience a warm and loving community, yet ...

In 2021 I became interested in living in a cohousing community. In cohousing you own your own house and participate in communal meals and activities in a common house. I had loved living communally at Porterhaus with Peter. I didn't have any community now. I wanted socialization and thought there were good communities out there. One directory listed over twelve hundred intentional communities in North America. I just happened to land in a cult.

Brenda and I discovered a cohousing community that was particularly attractive in Northampton Massachusetts. It was just a short walk across the Smith College campus to the funky downtown. We liked the house and many of the people who were already living in the cohousing village. But then I had an interview with one of the leaders, who had the unit across the way from the unit we were going for. After we talked for a short time, he said, "Well, that about covers the bases. Let's wrap up." He sounded like a cold-hearted leader, not empathic, purely business. A big red flag arose in my mind. This is not who I want as my next-door neighbor or leader.

As I was contemplating the possibility of moving into a cohousing community, I began to feel fatigued and lost interest in daily activities. This progressed to the point where I became depressed. My unconscious mind was so afraid of the idea of joining another unloving community that I fell into a deep depression. It came on quickly. At a core level I feared the trauma of spiritual abuse. I began to have suicidal ideation. It would be fine with me if I died. I thought my problems would be solved if I jumped in front of a local commuter train. Brenda and I recognized that something serious was going on with me. After conversing with my therapists on the phone and explaining my thoughts and behavioral symptoms, I arranged to enter McLean Psychiatric Hospital as a patient.

The buildings were old but dignified and venerable in their architecture, like an Ivy League college. The building where I would be housed was in a different, more private part of the McLean campus.

After I checked in, a senior staff person went through my small suitcase with me. She was a small, older woman with a gravelly voice. She pulled out my safety razor and said, "Nope."

My belt, "Nope." Even the charger for my phone, "Nope."

"When your phone needs a charge, you can drop it off at the office and we'll charge if for you. If you're on the list, you can check out a safety razor in the morning to shave."

"What list? What if I'm not on it?"

"Then you can't shave alone. A male staff person will go with you."

I went into the bathroom and noticed there were no regular faucets. You had to push the top down on the hot or cold faucet and water would come out of it for about five seconds. Same business with the shower, which was a pain because it never really heated up. When I went into the bathroom for my morning ablutions, I saw that there wasn't a shelf in the whole bathroom, and no hooks. You could get a clean towel, however.

We all had to wear face masks because of COVID. A psychiatrist came by daily to check on how I was doing with my meds. He was a bit formal with a heavy German accent. I had two roommates. One spoke only Spanish. The other was a very nice guy who had been there before and knew the ropes. His main problem was anxiety. The whole thing was weird, but I felt safe and warm.

Then my memory of the place gets quite sparse. For a reason. With my consent, I started receiving electroconvulsive therapy (ECT), otherwise known as shock therapy, which can alleviate depression but wipes out short-term memory. They would wheel me down to the ECT area, I'd get on a bed and a very nice nurse would hook up a few electrodes on my head, put an oxygen mask on me, and put a needle port in my arm to be ready for the administration of general anesthesia. I liked the smell of the bottled oxygen. It had a faint pine scent.

Then she'd wheel me into a smaller room with a kind doctor and an anesthesiologist. The anesthesiologist would put a needle into my port and ask me to count backward from ten. I was only able to count a few numbers. Then, it seemed like an instant later, I woke up in the recovery room and had some food and drink. I felt no pain, just very relaxed. It was over.

What they had done while I was out was to run a small current through a certain spot in my brain, just enough to induce a convulsion. They don't know why it works, but after ten treatments over about four weeks, it did cure my depression. It also wiped out my short-term memory, which was expected. For example, I only remember Brenda coming to visit me once; I think I wanted to play cards with her. But apparently, she came almost every day for the month of August. My long-term memory, however, was unaffected.

My depression was gone! So was any inclination to live in an intentional community of any kind. My trauma from the spiritual abuse I felt I experienced at Living Miracles ran deep. Now I felt mentally free of it.

I still felt bad about how, in my self-righteous way, I had discounted Melissa's feelings, divorced her by mail, and left her alone in our house with a lot of my stuff. She had a monumental job moving when she sold the house. Now that I was back in my right mind, I wrote this letter to her.

Dear Melissa,

I feel badly about how I left you in 2011. My intense study of ACIM and David Hoffmeister's teachings had warped my mind. I thought I would find the Love of God. I was hyper-focused on going to join the Living Miracles community and was not empathic with you. Ironically, I had written a book that was a guide to "true empathy." But I failed to practice it with you. I'm sorry. I also failed to practice it with myself and compromised my core values in order to join that community, which ended in a disaster of suicidal depression for me. You were right about David Hoffmeister's community all along. I was deceived.

I also apologize for how I ended our relationship in 2017. My email to you was much too abrupt, and I'm sorry for this, too.

You are a lovely person and I care about you.

Love,

Andy

Melissa replied almost immediately,

Dear Andy,

Thank you!

Through all those years I felt betrayed and invisible. I was exceedingly sad about the choices you made because I believed you already had what you appeared to be in search of and were unable to see it. I had made an unconscious bargain with myself that if I let you go you would come back. I hadn't allowed myself to know that time and experience would change everything.

I grieved again after I got that email. But I am a realist, and I worked very hard during those years to stay in the present and know that I am whole, even in the face of ruptured attachment.

I'm glad that you've found love. I hope your future is peaceful and full.

Love,

Melissa

I was very glad to have written that letter of apology. I had a bittersweet feeling reading her reply. Sad that I had treated her so badly and pleased that Melissa not only didn't hate me, but wished me well.

15.

My Son, Evan

Three years later, on November 12, 2021, I received a phone call from the human resources department of Amazon Web Services. They were calling because they were concerned that my son, Evan, had not shown up for his online work in three days. I felt a sudden icicle in my heart. Brenda and I drove to his condo in the Dorchester neighborhood of Boston. The blinds were drawn. I walked around back and managed to find a window that was not locked. I opened it and as I climbed through, I saw Evan lying on the floor on his left side, dead. His face was puffed and bluish and there was a small pool of dark-red blood on the floor from his left nostril. He was clutching his cellphone and something in his extended left hand. I let Brenda in through the back door.

I called 911 and reported the death and the address. The emergency dispatcher asked, "Is his body stiff?"

What the f...! I just found my dead son and you want me to try to see if his body moves!

I gently nudged his leg with my foot, reported he was stiff, and hung up. Then Brenda and I just collapsed into each other's arms crying. We cried and cried.

The police came and then people from the Medical Examiner's office. The police explained that what was in his left hand was

Narcan, an overdose medicine used to reverse the effects of opioids. Evan's possession of it indicated that he certainly was not trying to commit suicide. He was probably trying to reverse the effects of what he had taken. I imagined him desperately trying to save himself, passing out, and collapsing on the floor. I felt dizzy and held closely to Brenda's warm body as the two of us sobbed.

Months later, the Medical Examiner's report indicated that Evan died from fentanyl, a synthetic analgesic opioid fifty times more powerful than heroin, which had been mixed into whatever drug he was taking. Fentanyl death produces a rigid "fentanyl death pose," which I guess explains why the emergency dispatcher asked about rigidity of the body. It is highly addictive.

Illicitly manufactured fentanyl (IMF) is readily available on the drug market, often mixed in with other drugs, like methamphetamine, to increase the high as well as the addictive power. Once mixed, you can't see it, smell it, or taste it. It is deadly even in very tiny doses. The progression is sleepiness, passing out, and stopped breath. It is smuggled in from Mexico where it is manufactured in many clandestine labs. In 2021, 71,000 people died from fentanyl. It is the leading cause of death for people eighteen to forty-nine. U.S. border authorities are overwhelmed. The number of Americans killed by the drug jumped 94 percent from 2019 to 2021.

Evan was thirty-seven years old at the time and in many ways at the top of his game. He had been hired as a senior software developer in the training division of Amazon Web Services and was receiving $135,000 a year. His manager reported that Evan was making a strong contribution to the team. He had taken the job with the understanding that he would be training other people in person.

Unfortunately, because of COVID, he had to work in isolation at home and participate in meetings online.

To make his isolation worse, his social life had recently tanked. His girlfriend, Amelia, had left him and was now seeing his best friend, Liam. A double whammy. It affected him deeply. Evan was a people person, and he felt this loss keenly.

He had told me he was in emotional distress, and I invited him to come to dinner every Wednesday. A few days before his death, Brenda, Evan, and I had a great evening, each of us taking the Five Factor Model personality type instrument and comparing our results. We talked eagerly about the similarities in our different scores. We had a warm hug at parting.

Back in his Boston condo, however, Evan had to deal with his social pain and isolation alone. He also had to deal with chronic depression, general anxiety, and attention deficit disorder. I have the same psychological disorders. My psychiatrist prescribes venlafaxine for depression and general anxiety, methamphetamine for attention deficit disorder, and mirtazapine so I can get a good night's sleep. With these medications I experience the world as everyone else does.

Evan's sudden death shook the foundations of my belief that my life was working out all for the best. I had thought I had a sort of guardian angel when I was young, which only left me when I was depressed. Now I have brushed close to the black finality of death for the second time. I've largely gotten over the death by suicide of my elder brother, Tony, fifty-five years ago.

But I was the guy who discovered Evan's dead body on the floor. My son, whom I had loved since he was a baby, wrestled with on the rug, and nurtured through his growing years. His love for me was so strong that even after I had left for six years, he contacted me, said he loved me, and wanted to see me. Suddenly his body was dead and with it his personality, the essential presence of Evan in the room, was gone forever. I have been indelibly marked by Evan's death. I have become even quieter and more introverted.

One thing I have done to help me cope with Evans's loss is to begin writing. Telling Evan's story is a healing process. It allows me to bear witness to how wonderful his life was and how much he was loved. His sudden death is a powerful example to others who are not fully aware of the widespread presence and destructive power of fentanyl. I must write about his death as a warning to others. Our society needs to snap awake, to recognize the failure of the "war on drugs," and to develop broad, new life-affirming policies such that people don't have to resort to activity that puts them at risk of fentanyl death.

Evan was a great citizen and a good friend. He sought something deeper in life, a purpose that was meaningful and energizing. He found that purpose in two groups that helped people to attain their true potential. He joined Boston Toastmasters and was well known as an excellent public speaker. He held several official positions in Toastmasters and became the president. He enjoyed helping others to become better public speakers. I watched several of his talks on video and found them to be engaging, informative and uplifting.

He also joined Landmark Worldwide, a personal and professional growth, training and development company focusing on people achieving success, fulfillment, and greatness. He participated in many of their programs and helped others to do so. I suspect that his Landmark experience helped him to stop resenting me and encouraged him to write to me. Some of the phrasing of his letter to me sounded a bit like the way Landmark people spoke.

Evan had a loving soul and many friends. Framed next to his bed, he had this quotation from George Bernard Shaw's play *Man and Superman* (1903).

> This is the true joy in life, the being used for a purpose recognized by yourself as a mighty one; the being a force of nature instead of a feverish, selfish little clod of ailments and grievances complaining that the world will not devote itself to making you happy.
>
> I am of the opinion that my life belongs to the whole community, and as long as I live it is my privilege to do for it whatever I can.
>
> I want to be thoroughly used up when I die, for the harder I work the more I live. I rejoice in life for its own sake. Life is no "brief candle" for me. It is a sort of splendid torch which I have got hold of for the moment, and I want to make it burn as brightly as possible before handing it on to future generations.

Evan's torch burned brightly, and he became a torchbearer for his community. His life was a triumph of overcoming heroin addiction in the 1990s, rising high professionally as a software developer, and inspiring others to develop to their true potential through Toastmasters and Landmark. He was in good physical shape and ran 5K races.

After his death, we held a celebration of life ceremony for him at our Unitarian Universalist church. I spoke about how he had saved my life by helping me get out of Living Miracles. I met dozens of his friends for the first time and realized I didn't know a lot about the life he lived in Boston. I asked some of his friends to write something about him.

A woman he had gone to college with described this experience.

When I explained my story, Evan was deeply interested in all my thoughts, opinions, and experiences. I remember thinking that this was the first time in my life a male thought what I had to say was important. I remember feeling the validation in his true genuine interest.

Another friend from Toastmasters told me that one summer night he and Evan had driven their electronic scooters to the beach and talked late into the night about the ups and downs of their life stories. The friend said that for the first time, he felt fully understood and accepted by someone. "Your son made me feel like I belonged. I've felt better about myself, and better about my future, thanks to him."

Personally, Evan was kind and generous. He had many friends. He would invite groups of six to eight people up to our cabins on a pond in the Adirondacks for a week. He had an amusing knack for the dramatic. A friend shared that, upon arriving at the cabins, he addressed the group this way.

Gentlemen and ladies, listen closely now
for I have your attention for but a moment.

Let us pause and bathe ourselves in appreciation
for that which we now have to be joyful:
For the fondness of one another's company
For the natural beauty of this place
And for the talking, excitement, and fun
which shall soon emanate from these walls.
Pause in this, just for a moment, if you will
For it is these moments, these brief instances,
that are the fabric of our most cherished memories.

One of his friends wrote this about Evan.

His New Year's Eve parties were always fun. I appreciated that, while fun, there was some wholesomeness to them too. I felt safe. I didn't have to worry about drunk men taking advantage of me or people throwing up on me. I delighted in fun conversation, respectful dancing, and some finger foods and drinks. I felt comfortable bringing friends knowing they'd be taken care of and welcome in his environment. Evan and I both love bringing people together with parties. He'd come to mine when he could.

Evan's former girlfriend, Amelia, who was with Evan for several years, sent me this list of "fun facts" about him.

—Evan loved 90s music. He also loved music in general…from rock to indie to dance to top 40 teen hits. And he *loved* to dance.
—Evan's favorite movie was *The Remains of the Day*, starring Emma Thompson and Anthony Hopkins.

—He also loved to watch documentaries, particularly history-related, or relevant news. He talked to me at great length about a documentary that he had watched on the cult massacre at Jonestown. He also loved watching videos by the German YouTube channel *Kurzgesagt*, which runs a series called *In a Nutshell*. In the series they break down important, and sometimes hard to understand, subjects, such as: biology, the animal kingdom, physics, ethical dilemmas, and relevant current events and debates, in a precise, short, informative, and accessible way.

—Evan wanted to be a father.

—Evan enjoyed children and was always very interested in trying to communicate with them and discover what was going on in their lives.

—Evan always wished he had a sibling.

—Evan wanted to be a writer. He had a series of unfortunate life events hit him, one after another, including being let go from a job. One night he broke down in front of me and I comforted him, and we had a really long conversation. I asked him what he would do if he could do anything, and he said he wished he could write.

—Evan gave amazing speeches at Toastmasters. In fact, he was one of the few people who didn't constantly look at their notes when they were talking. He went on to become President.

—More than anything, Evan wanted to bring people together, and make a difference in people's lives.

—On the weekends, he *needed* people and social interactions. But during the week he liked some space to do the things he wanted to do.

—He was generous with his friends and would pay attention to little things. Whenever he knew he had people coming over, he would stock the fridge with their favorite beverage. Sometimes he would randomly send people pizzas to their house at night too.

—Evan was the one person that I knew I could be honest about my feelings with. He would listen to what I had to say, and really reflect on it. He would apologize without any prompting, and we could talk things out. Maybe not always at that moment, (though usually,) but we eventually would. Just that little thing about him always meant *so* much to me.

—He would sometimes leave me love notes on the mirror in the bathroom with a dry erase marker, for me to see in the morning.

—He really, really admired you and looked up to you. If there was a movie that you liked that you told him about, he would watch it. He would tell me about things that you had taught him as a child that he still remembered. When he would talk about himself, he would liken himself to you. He would say things like, "I'm [this way] and my dad is too." Or "I have [this personality trait] just like my dad." Or even, "I like this [subject] just like my dad."

Tears come to my eyes reading that last part about him wanting to be like me. I love him so much! When I think of losing Evan, I just want to scream "Damn!" or worse, and I often do. I wish he were still alive. Unless you have lost a child, it isn't possible to understand the magnitude of the loss. One way in which we are alike, and in which I am very proud of him, is that he was a loving person. This he demonstrated by his empathic listening skills, which several of his friends spoke about to me.

Every summer during his childhood I took him to the Adirondacks, often with his cousin, Will, for a fun time in the woods. We have two cabins up there on a wilderness pond. The three of us would have a great time sailing on the pond, swimming, canoeing, chopping down dead trees, building fires in the fireplace, and going on hikes up local mountains. Will reminded me of one windy day when we were racing our red sailboat along with the wind. The boys would chant together "We're making good speed, good speed." We went to come about and accidentally capsized the boat. They had their life preservers on and, far from a disaster, the boys were laughing as they clambered up and dove off the upturned hull of the boat. The next day wasn't as windy, so I let the boys take the sailboat out by themselves. They capsized it on purpose and had a riotous time in the water.

Can I have a meaningful life after losing Evan? I invested so many years of loving attention in him. I took parenting classes and went on to teach parenting classes to be sure I knew how to be a good father. At bedtime I used to read to him, from *Goodnight Moon* through *The Hobbit* and The Chronicles of Narnia. After I closed his door, I would play the few songs I knew on the alto recorder to lull him to sleep.

I compromised with his mother about custody to avoid a huge, prolonged fight and allowed him to go to school in her district rather than mine. This meant she had Evan during the week, and I had him on the weekends. Evan and I would take long bike rides, go skating, cross-country ski, and play all kinds of games. I arranged for him to play soccer in the local soccer league.

After attending Rutgers and Keene State College he lived and worked in Manchester, New Hampshire. I noticed he sometimes chose unwholesome people as friends. At Rutgers some of his "friends" got him to return some stolen books to the university bookstore. Evan was going to give them the money. Of course, the bookstore discovered right away that the books had been stolen and Evan was arrested. I was disappointed at what a stupid move that was, but it was an indication of how desperate he was to have friends. I regretted that he was an only child.

He had jobs as a web developer. He had some trouble with lateness; apparently his antidepressant medications made it hard to get up in the morning. I wonder if there was anything I could have done that would have kept him away from the bad drugs. Perhaps I could have done something if I hadn't left for six years.

In December 2018 after my return, I wanted to bring Evan and Brenda's children Julianna and Blake together with me for Christmas. Julianna, who hates the snow, was in her early thirties and was living in Tucson with her boyfriend Marshall. I offered to fly Brenda, Blake, and Evan to Tucson for a holiday visit. This was Evan's opportunity to meet Julianna. We stayed in a colorful little Mexican-style house with a fire pit we all sat around and talked in the evening.

The next day we all went hiking together in the desert in the Tucson mountains among the saguaro cactuses, which can easily be fifty feet high and 125 years old. Another day, I took Evan out because he had expressed interest in having a genuine cowboy hat. I took him all over Tucson trying on hats that either weren't quality-made or the right size. Finally, we found a beautiful black leather hat that fit him perfectly and I gave it to him as a Christmas present. Then we went to the Arizona Sonora Desert Museum with its world-renowned zoo, natural history museum and botanical garden.

Throughout our stay Evan got along easily and well with Brenda's children.

After our visit, Brenda, Evan, and I flew to Los Angeles, where we went to Universal Studios and The Wizarding World of Harry Potter. We got to ride on broomsticks for a simulated quidditch game. We went to dinner at the home of an old friend of mine from UCLA. Evan was happy to be with us throughout the whole adventure and we had a great time.

I think of Evan daily. If there are things growing in the yard that bring me joy, I want to show him. When there are dead trees to cut up, I think of him with his chainsaw, or the time he fixed the battery on my electric chainsaw. I keep several of the things Evan made around the house, such as a piece he welded to keep our cat from scratching the screen door, a coaster with the LeCompte coat of arms burned into it, and a plastic soap dish. Evan forged all kinds of plastic things with his 3D printer. Most of all I miss talking with him, hugging him, and telling him "I love you" whenever we separated. I hadn't realized the extent to which I had invested my life in him.

I am sorry that he never found a girl to marry. On one of his visits to our house Evan told me that Amelia had left him and was now in a relationship with his best friend. What he felt was this double betrayal hurt Evan a lot. He unfriended her and a few others on Facebook. I believe that if he had had a loyal loving woman at his side, Evan would not have lapsed back into taking drugs. It's tragic that someone as extroverted and loving as Evan lived alone.

Losing my one adult child devastated me. I expect for the rest of my life I will carry this dark pit of sadness, of feeling bereft, which comes up when I see other parent-child relationships, including

Brenda in loving interaction with her children Julianna and Blake. Blake is marrying a lovely young woman in Queens, NY, and I am so happy for them both. They will likely have children and I'm looking forward to that. I will be a step grandfather.

For several months I had a cynical take on the world, like I had nothing more to lose. It appeared that capitalist greed would lead to a climate catastrophe, an overheating of the planet, so great as to extinguish the human race. I was okay with that. It looked like the MAGA Republicans were poised to usher in fascist rule in the United States. It no longer bothered me. I just thought both of these catastrophes would be interesting to watch before I died.

My dark pit opens up when I visit with my niece and see her two beautiful, happy children, and remember Evan's death. Or I see photos of friends on Facebook with their grandchildren. Or I get together with my senior friends, and after talking about illnesses, the talk always gets around to "How are your kids doing?" If they don't already know, I tell them my son died. I prefer to be brief, as there is a stigma around death from drug overdose. Simply learning that my son is dead can bring other people down. I'm at grandparent age. But the LeCompte line will not continue. My circle of life is broken and will not go on. I buried my son Evan next to my brother, Tony. I would love there to be an afterlife where we could all be together.

I blame myself for having made a bad marriage with Emily, which led to divorce. I know our divorce hit Evan hard at the tender ages of two, three, and four. I regretted the custody agreement we had as he grew older. I wondered if his mother left Evan at home alone some evenings.

Dealing with his estate was a long and painful process. Emily drove up from South Carolina with her husband in an RV. Evan had provided well for her, leaving her his retirement account. He remembered me with his life insurance, which surprised me, given that I was away for six years. Brenda and I donated some things, and we did an estate sale to help clear out his condo to make it sale ready, putting the proceeds in a separate estate account. He had his whole condo wired with smart devices which could turn on the lights, music, unlock the door, set the temperature all from his phone. He had a great number of tools for welding, knife-making, leather working, 3D printing, computer building, speakers, and cameras. For transportation he had a car that looked like mine and an electronic scooter and skateboards.

There was so much for us to do to settle his estate. I am grateful that Brenda did so much, as I found it painful to see all the effects of his life disconnected from him. She arranged a number of sales and donations of his personal property. We couldn't sell his condo for over a year because the probate court took so long. By that time the market had gone from hot to cold and the price dropped by tens of thousands of dollars. We ended up with some of his pots and pans. Every time I use one, I think of how he always purchased high-quality items.

His letter to me, as I was being ejected by the Living Miracles community, lifted me up and gave me a loving way out. It was a miracle. I just wish he were still alive.

Now there are two headstones next to each other in the cemetery for the two men who loved me the most. One for my brother, Anthony Walker LeCompte, and one for my son, Evan Charles LeCompte.

16.

Soaring with Brenda

I think Evan's death would have thrown me into depression and suicide, were it not that my life has found purpose in my loving relationship with Brenda. She has always been there for me around Evan's death. We have had other losses. My wonderful psychotherapist, Fred Silverstone, died in the fall of 2021. Three of Brenda's brothers, Donald, David, and Mario, all died within a year and a half. Despite all this loss, with our strong love for each other, we feel secure and strong in the world. As Brenda puts it, we can both feel great sadness, as well as great joy.

Brenda grew up the oldest daughter in a family of eight children. Her mother suffered from a serious illness and was frequently out of action for extended periods of time. Most of her siblings had different fathers. The records show that she went to fifteen different elementary schools! Her mother kept Brenda as a virtual slave in charge of cooking and taking care of all the others. They settled down in Chicago and Brenda attended Lakeview High School. She grew to be an extremely attractive young woman and was named the Queen of Hollywood/Ardmore Beach for an air and water show. A perceptive music teacher identified that Brenda had a beautiful voice. Brenda sang a solo from *Fiddler on the Roof* to an audience of over a thousand at the high school.

Brenda was married to a medical doctor of alternative medicine until his unfortunate death in 2012. After a period of grieving, she began to sing again at open mics in the western suburbs of Boston. With her warm and kind personality her circle of musical friends grew. After five years or so she was motivated to look for another partner. We connected online in 2017 and met for dinner on August 23.

I moved in with Brenda on November 1, 2017. She is the best companion in the world. My life with her is fun. She says what she is thinking, which often turns out to be what I am thinking. She is passionate. We hug and kiss many times a day. We cuddle every night.

We have the same love language priorities. The five love languages are five different ways of expressing and receiving love: words of affirmation, quality time, receiving gifts, acts of service, and physical touch. We order them this way 1) physical touch 2) quality time 3) words of affirmation 4) acts of service and 5) receiving gifts. We have the same Myers-Brigs personality type: ENFP.

One thing about myself that I didn't know before Brenda was how much I wanted and enjoyed giving and receiving love. I had never experienced it when I was young. Now it is the best part of being alive.

We love each other delightedly. I am delighted every time she wants to hug and kiss. She is delighted every time I want to hug and kiss. These times turn out to be mutually desired by each of us at the same time. I love it. She feels so good to hold. She is the most emotionally intelligent person I have ever met. Her intuition about people is astonishingly accurate. She helps me communicate with others, write emails, and schedule our social life. She is very considerate of my every feeling. We are both into people-pleasing, big time!

Our harmonious relationship is living proof of the truth I laid out in my book *Creating Harmonious Relationships*. We meet each other's hopes for freedom and connection on a daily basis, hardly having to think about it. This true empathy is the foundation of interpersonal love.

After we had been together for a year, a friend sent us information about a weeklong singing program, the Tuscany Project, and Brenda and I decided to do it. We flew to Italy and spent several days in Florence before the start of the project. We walked all over Florence and saw Botticelli's *Birth of Venus* at the Uffizi Gallery. We saw Michelangelo's *David* at the Galleria dell' Accademia and had our pictures taken on the Ponte Vecchio bridge. We visited outdoor cafes, saw street artists, and encountered happy, friendly people. We enjoyed a very kind, informative host at our B&B.

We then rented a car and joined the Tuscany Project at a restored twelfth-century villa located on a secluded hillside near the town of Perugia. The property includes an infinity swimming pool with a panoramic view of the entire valley. On a terrace, we savored meals emphasizing local culinary traditions with organic vegetables and aromatic herbs from the kitchen garden.

Participants came together from all over the world in a noncompetitive environment to celebrate each person's unique voice and story. We had the joy of learning in a vibrant community of people. Three outstanding teachers combined their skills as musicians, actors, singers, and teachers to create our artistic singing retreat.

I chose John Denver's "Poems, Prayers and Promises" to sing

225

because it reflected my newfound satisfaction with my life, with who I really am, a loving man full of gratitude. The lyrics that clinched it for me are: "How sweet it is to love someone, How right it is to care." These lines reflect the reversal in my mind. I sought love in the abstract and couldn't find it. But Brenda's love for me, and my love for her, have been truly transformative.

After the retreat we visited the medieval town of Gubbio and went to the top of the mountain in a funicular. I made a video as we ascended and put it to the tune of "Funiculì, Funiculà!" Then we visited Assisi and saw where St. Francis founded his monastic order. We got along famously well, and it was the perfect vacation.

Our friends say they enjoy seeing us together, that we are in such harmony. We enjoy taking walks together in the woods, every day if we can. We are fine with each other doing his or her own thing during the day. Brenda decorates the house with fresh flowers. I like to chop vegetables and clean up after dinner, with special attention to the pots and pans. I hang out with my friend John Heymann and take longer hikes. Brenda and I enjoy doing things together like biking and kayaking. We also enjoy just being home.

When I moved into Brenda's house, I became a vegan overnight. Brenda had been a vegan for years. I welcomed this life change to improve my well-being. We both wanted to improve our health and lose some weight. Together we have sought out plant-based eating and minimized processed carbohydrates. Brenda chooses whole-food recipes and prepares delicious meals. We attend regular plant-based potlucks with a group of vegans and "vegan-curious" people connected with the Unitarian Universalist Church. The group also strives, through our diets, to reverse the climate dangers associated with beef production and commercial fishing.

Brenda enjoys creating and maintaining a beautiful home that is warm, welcoming, and fun.

She doesn't nag me. There are times when I'm just lying around being a slug reading the news and Brenda just lets me be. We are lovingly accepting of the other and don't feel a need to change the other. Our love is a strong force that has created a peaceful and easy relationship.

And I found teaching again. I have been teaching English as a second language, offering individual tutoring and on-line and in-person classes at the local library. I find it fun and very satisfying to teach both beginning and advanced students. I take delight in finding articles and talks that are of interest and at the appropriate level for my students. Most of my students are Asian and I recently got my first refugee, a grandmother still wearing a cast on her arm from the Russian bombing of Mariupol, Ukraine.

Brenda and I wanted to share our love and happiness with our family and friends and have our wedding be a public celebration demonstrating that true love was possible, even in our sixties and seventies. Because of the COVID pandemic, we re-scheduled our wedding three times.

Brenda and I were married in the Italian Garden at the Codman Estate in Lincoln, Massachusetts on June 12, 2022. The day before, a 60 percent chance of rain was forecasted. But the rain held off and it turned out to be a perfect day. Friends provided lovely music on guitar and violin, and they accompanied us as we all sang "Give Yourself to Love" by Kate Wolf. Brenda sang Bob Dylan's "Make You

Feel My Love" to me. We lit a candle for Evan and Brenda's brothers so their spirits would be with us.

Our vows were:

I take you to be my best friend, my partner in life and my one true love.
All I want is to love you for the rest of my life,
to wake up every morning with you by my side,
knowing that whatever happens, you'll be there for me.
I will forever be there to laugh with you, to lift you up when you are down,
and to love you unconditionally through all the adventures of our life together.
You are my happiness. I love you.

We had a reception on the lawn of the estate. We invited fifty guests for a vegan dinner and dancing in the beautiful old barn-like carriage house. After the nonalcoholic toast, we introduced everyone, which helped create the experience of an intimate, loving, and warm wedding. Then in July we had a party near our home to include more friends in the celebration of our marriage.

Brenda loves people. She often stops and talks to strangers. I may feel a little sad or jealous sometimes about the love Brenda sheds on her son and daughter, especially after Evans's death. But then I realize that her love includes me and that I feel it and benefit from it.

I feel so happy having married the most wonderful woman in the world for me. I marvel at Brenda's innocence. She is remarkable in that she takes what I say literally, which means I have to be more aware of what I say, including correcting my sarcasm. I see her always wanting to do the good thing, the right thing, the loving thing, and it amazes me. I think I'm becoming a more loving person by being with her.

Our interactions are almost always peaceful and calm. Brenda has a good sense of priorities and doesn't take issue with unimportant things. For example, not long ago I said, "These apples are bruised, one badly bruised. Check 'em over, and don't buy them if they're bruised."

Her playful response was, "Okay, I'll be more careful. You're the boss."

She doesn't have a petty ego to defend; on the contrary, she brings joy to our interactions. She does what she wants, a major component of which is to make me happy.

It feels as though I was made to be Brenda's partner in a loving relationship. And she feels that she was made for me. We are living proof that a loving interpersonal relationship brings great happiness and peace of mind.

Miracle found. Hallelujah, amen!

A Useful Skill for Getting Your Friend or Family Member Out of a Cult

THE PROBLEM

A person who joins a cult is in search of something that wasn't readily provided for them earlier in their families or among their friends and associates. This person had a desire that wasn't met to connect, to belong, to experience attention and approval from others, especially from parental figures such as a group leader. Initially, the cult satisfies this desire. Most cults ask the person to break off connections with their friends and family. This is to isolate the person from outside influences, allowing the cult to work on controlling the person's mind.

Most likely the person you know in a cult has been the victim of mind control. Cults use mind control to change people's thoughts and opinions. It leaves the person you are trying to save, the victim, in the position of believing what the cult says about itself. Mind control reinterprets the attempts of others to get them out as not true or evilly motivated. This creates a high hurdle for friends and family that is difficult to surmount without connecting at a heart level with the victim. Much time may pass, and hard feelings may arise in an attempt to deprogram the victim directly. Cult members are on guard and have been schooled against connecting with nonbelievers.

I propose an effective strategy that involves making a genuine connection with the victim at a heart level.

Having read *Finding Miracles: Escape from a Cult* it should be apparent that I wanted to leave the cult years before I actually left, because I wasn't sure I had a loving place to go. It was my son's letter that opened me to coming home. The letter he wrote was well thought out, convincing me that he loved me and that he genuinely wanted me to come home to Massachusetts. I visited my sister for a weekend before moving back to Massachusetts to see what my reception would be. I was aware that I was a psychological basket case, suffering from spiritual and emotional trauma, and probably functioning at a lower cognitive level. I wanted a safe place to be where I would receive tender loving care and guidance back into the world. Talking with my son and sister that weekend was sufficient to let me know it would be a safe place.

Your cult victim is afraid of leaving the cult because it has become their identity, their entire life-support system. They need to connect with someone they trust who can show them a better way.

A SOLUTION

Establish trust through genuine, heartfelt connection with the victim. This happens with communication in person, on the phone, or by email. If you can arrange a mutual time to meet, in-person communication, with a hug if appropriate, is the most powerful. Telephone is the next-best method, although it lacks visual cues. Emails can be effective if they are carefully designed to elicit the genuine feelings and hopes of the victim.

A direct way to establish a heartfelt connection is to use compassionate communication. Compassionate communication has four basic elements: fact, feeling, hope, and request. The use of use these four elements is described in detail in my earlier book, *Creating Harmonious Relationships: A Practical Guide to the Power of True Empathy.*

Here is one example of how the compassionate communication process might start:

You	Person in Cult
Opener: Is this a good time to talk?	Yes

Fact: When you entered (name of cultic organization

Feeling: I felt sad

Hope: Because I have valued our close relationship and wanted to keep it.

Request: Would you be willing to talk to me about what you were looking for when you joined?

The conversation would continue, with you helping them to state or guess their feelings and hopes. Hopes are universal, what everyone really wants. We hope for our own personal mix of hopes for connection and hopes for freedom, which vary depending on current circumstances.

Freedom Hopes

To have our own thoughts and opinions

To have our own feelings

To have our own intentions

To choose how we will spend our time

To have our own values

To have our own dreams, goals, and aspirations

To say what we think and feel

To express our creativity

To experience privacy, order, and psychological safety

To be treated with honesty

To be respected

Connection Hopes

To be heard and understood

To have our thoughts considered by others

To be accepted by others

To be appreciated

To experience harmony with others

To experience closeness and intimacy

To be supported

To be trusted

To love and be loved

To experience communion

To help others get their hopes met

To discuss ways to get your loved one out of a cult or discuss a relevant issue with the author, you may go to the author's website at:

AndrewLeCompte.com

Acknowledgments

I am deeply indebted to the following readers and advisors for help refining my manuscript.

- Brenda Asis – sensitivity reader, whose keen insight into people's psychology led me to some very valuable revisions.
- Katie Bannon – developmental editor, helped me improve my writing and put it in order.
- Daphne Blount – reader, clinical social worker/therapist.
- Gerette Buglion – author of *An Everyday Cult,* co-founder of #IGotOut where cult survivors tell their stories in a healing process. Provided me with long-term support.
- Dr. Stephen Hassan – a cult expert who encouraged me to write truthfully about my cult experience and have the courage to name the cult leader and the cult.
- Mary Christen – reader, social worker, offered insightful feedback.
- Aimeé Christian – writing teacher at GrubStreet Creative Writing Center, taught me the form and craft of memoir writing.
- Amy Eastwood – reader, first copy editor.
- Phyllis Evan – reader, enthusiast, who couldn't put it down and stayed up half the night.
- Artemis Joukowsky – author, filmmaker, and socially

conscious venture capitalist. Codirector, with Ken Burns, of the companion PBS documentary film *Defying the Nazis: The Sharps' War*. I am grateful for his enthusiasm regarding my manuscript and its promotion.

- Adam Hay – cover design, master of his craft; took an old photo of me and made a dramatic cover.
- John Heymann – developmental editor, thoroughly read the manuscript twice, pointing out all sorts of improvements.
- Marte Smith-Marston – reader, who offered meaningful commentary.
- Michael and Debbie Milburn – readers; Michael Milburn, PhD in social psychology, is founder and chief science officer at Impairment Science, Inc.
- Matthew Young – website and resource development, designed and built the AndrewLeCompte.com website and added some great resources.

Cult Recovery Resources

WEBSITES

AndrewLeCompte.com/resources Andrew LeCompte's website

Freedom of Mind Dr. Steven Hassan maintains this highly informative resource site, covering essential topics including Undue Influence and his BITE model of Authoritarian Control.

The Cult Education Institute Rick Alan Ross has assembled one of the largest archives of information about controversial groups, some called "cults," and related information.

IndoctriNation is a weekly podcast in which Rachel Bernstein sits down with former cult members, intervention experts, and people who have left narcissistic and controlling relationships of all kinds to hear their stories and discuss their past experience.

Cult Recovery 101 Cult Recovery associates are consultants, psychotherapists, and counselors with specialized training and experience, many of whom themselves are former cultists or have been exposed to destructive cults or other coercive influence techniques.

Janja Lalich and the Lalich Center on Cults and Coercion Janja

Lalich, PhD is an authority on cults, extremism, and coercion. She specializes in self-sealing, or closed, systems, with a particular focus on recruitment, indoctrination, and methods of influence and control. Learn about social-structural, social-psychological, and interpersonal behavioral patterns commonly found in cultic environments to help yourself assess a particular group or relationship.

Navigating Narcissism with Dr. Ramani In this podcast, Dr. Ramani Durvasula talks to survivors and experts to break down classic narcissistic patterns like manipulation, control, gaslighting, and love bombing and help unpack feelings of betrayal, shame, confusion, pain.

Cult Information Centre CIC was the first charitable organization established in the United Kingdom focusing critical concern on the harmful methods of the cults. CIC is concerned about the use of deceptive and manipulative methods used by cults to recruit and indoctrinate unsuspecting members of society.

A Little Bit Culty Think you might be in a cult? Want to know the signs? In their podcasts, Sarah Edmondson and Anthony "Nippy" Ames do a deep dive into how devotion can turn to dysfunction. (see the critically acclaimed HBO series *The Vow*)

iGotOut.org The mission of #igotout is to inspire survivors of high-demand environments who have experienced cultic, religious, or spiritual abuse to tell and share their stories, if and when it's safe to do so learn from each other and educate the public.

Dare to Doubt A resource hub for people detaching from harmful belief systems. The goal is to help people heal from the damage of indoctrination by connecting them with mental health professionals, aid organizations, and support groups.

International Cultic Studies Association The ICSA is a global network of people concerned about psychological manipulation and abuse in cultic environments. They have moved operations to Facebook.

BOOKS

Dr. Steven Hassan:
—*Combating Cult Mind Control: The Number One Best Selling Guide to Protection, Rescue, and Recovery from Destructive Cults. Park Street Press 1990*
—*Freedom of Mind. Helping Loved Ones Leave Controlling People, Cults, and Beliefs*, Freedom of Mind Press 2013
—*Releasing the Bonds: Empowering People to Think for Themselves*, Freedom of Mind Press 2000
—*The Cult of Trump: A Leading Cult Expert Explains How the President Uses Mind Control*, Free Press 2019.

Captive: A Mother's Crusade to Save Her Daughter from a Terrifying Cult by Catherine Oxenberg, Gallery Book, 2018.

Scarred: The True Story of How I Escaped NXIVM, the Cult That Bound My Life by Sarah Edmondson, Chronicle Prism 2019. Dramatic firsthand account.

Cults Inside Out: How People Get In and Can Get Out by Rick Alan Ross, CreateSpace Independent Publishing Platform 2014. Comprehensive and scholarly.

Losing Reality: on Cults, Cultism, and the Mindset of Political and Religious Zealotry, by Robert J. Lifton, The New Press 2019. Lifton is a psychiatrist and author best known for his studies of the psychological causes and effects of war and political violence and for his theory of thought reform and cult behavior.

Fr. Benedict J. Groeschel, *A Still, Small Voice: A Practical Guide on Reported Revelations*, Ignatius Press, San Francisco, 1993. Groeschel, an expert on the para-normal, knew Helen Schucman well.

Janja Lalich, *Take Back Your Life: Recovering from Cults and Abusive Re-lationships,* written with Madeline Tobias, 2006. Audio book narrated by Sarah Edmondson. Audiobooks 2021

Two documentaries on an ACIM-related Cult, Endeavor Academy

The Academy: Miracle Or Cult?
Miracles happen at the Endeavor Academy in Wisconsin Dells, Wisconsin.
Leaving Endeavor Academy
Dec 6, 1999 — Anderson took the New-Age doctrine of a *A Course in Miracles* and twisted its principles of self-enlighten-ment.

A Course in Miracles All quotes are from *A Course in Miracles*,

ARTICLES

"The Curious Mystical Text Behind Marianne Williamson's Presidential Bid"
The New Age author was drawn to an esoteric bible in the 1970s. It made her a self-help megastar. And now it has gone mainstream. By Sam Kestenbaum – *New York Times* July 5, 2019

A Course in Brainwashing, Tracy Moran. June 2, 1996, issue of Our Sunday Visitor. Our Sunday Visitor, Inc, 200 Noll Plaza, Huntington, In 46750.

A Course in Miracles by Edward R Hryczyk, A step-by-step critique of ACIM in Dialogue Ireland, an independent trust that works to promote awareness and understanding of religious issues and cultism in Ireland. Dialogue Ireland contains additional articles on ACIM.

The Definitive Guide to Helping People Trapped in a Cult, Dr. Steven Hassan, *Psychology Today* April 2021

How to Get Someone Out of a Cult By Malia Wollan, *New York Times Magazine*, September 26, 2018

Cults Are Going Virtual, but Deprogramming Needs one Old-School

Tactic, asking a question. *Inverse*, Elizabeth Svoboda, August 17, 2021

ABOUT THE AUTHOR

ANDREW LECOMPTE

With a master's degree in Humanistic Psychology in Organizations, Andrew developed a deeper method of interpersonal communication, which involves tapping into each person's emotions and what they are most hoping for. He then taught empathic speaking and listening skills to people in schools, colleges, civic groups, legal practices, hospitals, pharmaceutical and financial corporations. As president of the Let's Talk training group he led leadership, management, and organizational development programs. Andrew wrote a book encapsulating this way of communicating: *Creating Harmonious Relationships: a Practical Guide to the Power of True Empathy* (2000). The initial book sold out five thousand copies and was translated into Turkish. A Revised Edition is launching in January 2024.

In the spiritual realm, Andrew began meditating in the 1970s. In the 1990s, he began studying the spiritual text, *A Course in Miracles* (ACIM). In 2004 he met the man who would become his ACIM guru/teacher. Andrew discussed key points of ACIM with his wife, a clinical psychologist, who was not in agreement with a spiritually focused life. In 2011, listening to the persuasions of the teacher, Andrew left his family and friends, and all his possessions behind and moved two thousand miles into his teacher's ACIM-based community. There he contributed his teaching and counseling skills, plus his book-editing and video-editing skills. But after six grueling years he realized it was a cult and escaped. Cult psychology is a pernicious force. With the help and love of his family Andrew devoted himself to intensive recovery programs. After researching cults and cult psychology he wrote this memoir *Finding Miracles: Escape from a Cult.*

Andrew LeCompte may be reached through his website:

AndrewLeCompte.com

If you enjoyed reading this book, please post an honest review on Amazon to help fellow readers find books that appeal to them.